the top 13 questions about GOD

Intense Discussions
For Youth Ministry

Group
Loveland, Colorado

Group resources actually work!

This Group resource incorporates our R.E.A.L. approach to ministry. It reinforces a growing friendship with Jesus, encourages long-term learning, and results in life transformation, because it's

Relational
Learner-to-learner interaction enhances learning and builds Christian friendships.

Experiential
What learners experience through discussion and action sticks with them up to 9 times longer than what they simply hear or read.

Applicable
The aim of Christian education is to equip learners to be both hearers and doers of God's Word.

Learner-based
Learners understand and retain more when the learning process takes into consideration how they learn best.

"I am sending you out like sheep among wolves. Therefore be as shrewd as snakes and as innocent as doves."
— Matthew 10:16

The Top 13 Questions About God: Intense Discussions for Youth Ministry

Copyright © 1998 and 2002 Group Publishing, Inc.

2002 edition

Visit our Web site: **group.com**

Credits
Contributing Authors: Bob Buller, Jan Kershner, Steve Saavedra, Amy Simpson, Michael D. Warden, and Paul Woods
Editor: Karl Leuthauser
Chief Creative Officer: Joani Schultz
Copy Editor: Janis Sampson
Art Director: Ray Tollison
Computer Graphic Artist: Randy Kady
Cover Art Director: Jeff A. Storm
Cover Designer: Lisa Chandler
Production Manager: Dodie Tipton

Library of Congress Cataloging-in-Publication Data
The Top 13 Questions About God: Intense Discussions for Youth Ministry
    p.   cm.
   ISBN 978-0-7644-2426-7
   1. God-Proof-Juvenile literature.   I. Group Publishing.
BT107.S79 1998
268'433-dc21

98-5947
CIP

18 17 16 15 14 13   11 10 09 08

Printed in the United States of America.

Contents

Introduction

We're Not Going to Lose Them Anymore

"I was raised in the church, but there are just so many things about the Christian faith I find so unbelievable. How could a loving God send people to hell? Why does he allow so much pain on earth? There are millions of Muslims in the Middle East who believe in Allah with all their hearts. Are you going to tell me that they're all *wrong?*"

So many of the young adults in our youth groups return from their first year in the "real" world downcast and doubting. Ask anyone you know who grew up in the church and has fallen away from the Christian faith why he or she doesn't trust and believe in Jesus Christ. The person will either point to the behavior of Christians or to one of the questions found in this book. Is the message of the gospel so illogical? Is Christian morality and truth so stale and easily forgotten? Why are we losing the ones we have worked so hard to bring to Jesus?

Whether you're a youth pastor or a volunteer youth worker, your group must *prepare* for the philosophical onslaught that is soon to come. This book offers the opportunity to help your students grapple with the big questions of Christianity in a safe Christian environment. Christianity is not illogical, irrelevant, or untrue. The discussions in this book will help your group see how rational and vitally important Christianity is today. Use this book to prepare your group. We're not going to lose them anymore.

How to Use This Book

Before each meeting, photocopy the Christian perspective, the "Faith Challenge" page, and the "My Response" page for each person.

This book is designed to provide the "substance" of your meetings. You may want to begin your meeting with food, drinks, and fellowship. For the last ten minutes of the food time, have group members read the Christian perspective of the lesson and complete the journaling section that follows. If you don't have time to do this during your meeting, have group members complete the reading and journaling before the meeting. You might also want to suggest that everyone in your group memorize the Scripture following the journaling section before the meeting. But if you have time, have group members memorize the Scripture during the meeting. Test each other on the Scripture throughout the meeting time.

Then use the rest of the lesson to lead discussion. Before you start discussion, you may want to set down some rules. You can come up with these as a group or use the following suggestions.

- Only one person in each group should be talking at any given time.
- You are welcome to disagree, but please don't argue or fight.
- Never attack a person for his or her opinion.
- Listen before you speak.
- It's OK to say "I don't know."
- If the leader changes plans or interrupts a discussion, be flexible.

Before the discussion, pray that God will help you understand and find his truth. Ask God to take your group where he wants it to go.

During your discussions, you may encounter difficult questions that no one in your group can answer. When this happens, encourage your students to investigate the questions through outside reading, prayer, studying Scripture, discussion with their pastor, discussion with their parents, or discussion with respected adults in your church. Make sure you follow up on the question the following week. It's OK to have questions about faith, but it's foolish to let the questions linger without a sincere attempt at finding accurate answers.

But sometimes it takes a considerable amount of time and study before you arrive at an answer that satisfies the question. As your students search and wait, help them remember the prayer that one man said to Jesus, "I do believe; help me overcome my unbelief!" (Mark 9:24).

"You can keep a faith only as you can keep a plant, by rooting it into your life and making it grow there."[1]
—Phillips Brooks

As you help people overcome the intellectual challenges they have regarding Christianity, some group members may want to become Christians or reaffirm their commitment to Christ. To help a person do this, consider using the following model.

- Admit that you are a sinner in need of forgiveness.
- Acknowledge that Jesus paid the price for your sins through his death.
- Ask God to forgive you for your sins.
- Tell God that you want him to take control of your life and that you give him control of your life.
- Thank God for forgiving you and making you his child.
- Tell someone about the steps you took and why you took them.
- Talk to your pastor about what it means to belong to a church.

If circumstances arise in your group that you feel are inappropriate or out of control, notify your pastor as soon as possible. If a group member reveals suicidal thoughts, physical or sexual abuse, or identifies himself or herself as a runaway, consult your pastor immediately.

It is our prayer that this book will help you and the members of your group come to truly know Jesus, to put your trust in him, and to come to an understanding of why you believe what you believe.

1. How Can I Know God Exists?

INDIVIDUAL WORK
One Christian Perspective to Think About

OK. This is a biggie. This issue is one that everyone deals with and that can pretty much determine the way you live every day.

So how can we know that God exists? We can't see or touch God. And sometimes we think we can't even see evidence of God's presence in the world. And for many of us, if we can't see, touch, and prove beyond all doubt that something exists, then sorry—it just doesn't exist.

A lot of people have a lot to say on this subject. Christianity traditionally holds to three naturalistic arguments for the existence of God.

The cosmological argument—This argument basically says that God must exist because the universe exists. The universe around us must have a cause, and God is the cause—the most adequate explanation for the existence of the universe. Since something can't come from nothing, there must be a creator out there responsible for making the world. At the least, believing in God requires no more faith than believing the world came into existence in some other way. In fact, it takes less faith because it makes the most sense (see Genesis 1:1–2:3).

The teleological argument—This one goes beyond the *existence* of the universe, focusing on the *kind* of universe we live in. Our world and the creatures, systems, and structures in it are amazing. The genetic code in DNA molecules is incredibly complex. The balance of the earth in space is precisely what it needs to be to sustain human life. The food chain, the rotation of the earth, and the intricate systems of the human body all point to a designer who created the universe for a purpose. According to this argument, there must be a God who created the world we live in. It couldn't have come into being by chance (see Psalm 19:1-6).

The anthropological argument—This argument focuses on humanity and the way *we're* made. As you look around the universe, it should be obvious that humans have abilities, thoughts, and other attributes that the rest of creation doesn't have. One thing that makes humans unique is their longing to know who they are, why they're here, and where they came from. Humans also have a sense of right and wrong—a conscience. Humans form support groups, write, draw, start revolutions, commit suicide, read, calculate complex math formulas, and invent new technological tools. Our intricate makeup points to a God who has created humans in his image. We ourselves provide evidence of God's existence because we exhibit some of God's nature every day (see Psalm 139:13-16).

So can we prove beyond all doubt that God exists? Of course not. If we could, he wouldn't be much of a God because he would be subject to the time, space, and logic we live within. God is not material, or physical, as we are. God doesn't have the limitations of material form. The fact that God is a far superior being makes it necessary that we can't fully understand him.

Fortunately, God has chosen not to leave us totally in the dark about his existence or his character. God actively works in the world he has created and in the lives of people. God relates to us as creator, ruler, judge, deliverer, and Father (for more on this, see Genesis 1:3–2:25; 3:8-24; Deuteronomy 1:29-31; Acts 14:11-17; 1 Corinthians 4:4-5; and even Galatians 3:25-27). The fact that God does relate to us in personal ways helps to solidify our faith in his existence.

Nevertheless, belief in God requires faith, just as every other explanation of the universe's existence, the design of the universe, and the nature of humanity requires faith. But that faith can be based on logical arguments from what we know and see every day.[1]

My Thoughts, Feelings, and Questions

Write your answers on the back of this paper.

● Has there ever been a time in your life when you questioned the existence of God? If so, what were the circumstances surrounding that time and what were your questions?

● If you've never questioned God's existence, how do you feel about your friends who have?

● Read John 1:1-5. What does this Scripture tell you about the existence of God and the existence of everything else?

Commit It to Memory

"In the beginning was the Word, and the Word was with God, and the Word was God."—John 1:1

QUESTIONS TO TALK ABOUT AS A GROUP

When everyone has read the Christian perspective and completed the journaling section, discuss these questions as a group.

- What are some things that seem to indicate that God doesn't exist?
- What do you think of the claim that if we could prove that God exists, he wouldn't be much of a God?
- What do you think it would take for everyone in the world to become completely convinced that God exists?
- Read Romans 1:18-25 and Psalm 19:1-6. How can we be certain of God's existence according to these Scripture passages?
- What are a few of the reasons people doubt the existence of God according to these verses?
- What does "futile" thinking look like today?
- Why do you think many people prefer gods they can see, feel, hear, and touch?
- What are some modern false gods?

SMALL-GROUP WORK

Give each student a copy of the "Faith Challenge" handout (p. 12). Ask youth to form small groups of three to five students. In their groups, have students read the challenging perspectives on the handout and discuss the questions that follow each one.

Jump-Start

If your group discussion needs a jump-start, read the following quotations and discuss the questions as a group.

"God is what man finds that is divine in himself. God is the best way man can behave in the ordinary occasions of life, and the farthest point to which man can stretch himself."[2]—Max Lerner

- Is there a limit to how much humans can improve?
- Can humans eventually become godlike?
- Can divinity and evil reside in the same being? If so, how do you think Lerner would explain the evil in people?

"We cannot get away from God, though we can ignore Him."[3]—James Elliott Cabot

- What are some of the ways people try to ignore God?
- Why do you think people are so eager to write God out of the equation of life?
- What would a godless society look like?

FAITH CHALLENGE
How Should Christians Respond to the Following Argument?

The concept of God is irrelevant because it has very little to do with liberating humanity from suffering, which is our greatest need as people. The way to reach this liberation is by following the Eightfold Path of Buddhism, a set of guidelines for right living. In Buddhist thought religious theories and theologies are meaningless. Believe in God if you wish—or don't. It really doesn't matter. As Gautama wisely teaches: "Let us avoid the confusing and controversial concept of God, of divinity, and let us immediately work toward the divination of humanity."[4]

● What do you think about the concept that all of us are our own gods?

● Do you agree or disagree with the claim that humans should work toward their fullest potential? Explain.

● Is God relevant to the suffering of humanity? Explain.

● Read Matthew 22:37-40. According to this passage, what's the purpose of our existence? How is this fundamentally different from the Buddhist understanding of life?

How Should Christians Respond to the Following Argument?

God is an obsolete idea that's no longer useful in a scientific world. Evolution has explained the processes that we once attributed to an unseen intelligence we erroneously called "God." The truth is that the only eternal thing in the universe is matter—not God. Matter has always existed. At one point, the matter that existed exploded in the big bang. This matter blew apart and spread throughout the universe. Eventually it cooled, forming suns, stars, planets, and moons. The matter that became the earth eventually formed the stuff of life—primitive life-forms. These life-forms began to evolve and develop into more advanced life-forms. After millions of years, they had evolved into plants, animals, and human beings. Life continues to evolve into higher forms, but the process is mostly undetectable because it takes so much time. This process of evolution is subject to laws and trends in the universe and does not require a supernatural being to guide it.

● Does the fact that there are natural laws in the universe (for example, the sun rises every morning) exclude the possibility of God's existence? Why or why not?

● Read Genesis 1:1–2:3. How does this creation story differ from the theory of evolution? How is it similar?

● What would you say to a friend who put his or her faith in evolution instead of God?

● Does the Bible address issues of science? Explain.

● Is it possible to believe in God and evolution at the same time? Explain.

Pair Share

Write the following questions on newsprint or a dry-erase board where everyone can see them. Ask teenagers to form pairs and discuss the questions with their partners.

- Why do you think people question God's existence?
- Which of these reasons can you relate to personally, if any?
- Tell your partner about a time you were tempted to doubt God's existence and explain why. Then think of things in which you see evidence of God's existence.
- Are there areas of your life (for example, your leisure time, your habits, and your thoughts) that have not fully come to terms with an ever-present, living God?

Group Work

Pray by name for the people you know who are struggling with the question of God's existence. Ask God to pursue them and reveal himself in a personal way.

Closing

Give each student a copy of the "My Response" handout (p. 14). Encourage youth to write out their prayers in response to God, using the prayer-starter on the handout. Then point out the action plans they can do in response to what they've learned in this lesson.

After time for personal prayer, you may want to finish the lesson with a group prayer.

My Response
My Response
Prayer

Dear God: Help me to be more aware of your existence and presence throughout the whole of life. Help me to…

_____

_____

_____

Action Plans

Try these ideas for putting what you've talked about into action.

● Take a walk through a park or a hike through the outdoors to ponder how God's glory is reflected in his creation.

● Keep a journal to record the times God has intervened in your life and made his presence known.

● If you intellectually doubt the existence of God, don't be afraid to discuss it with other people. Most people welcome such meaningful conversation. For example, engage in a heart-to-heart discussion with your leader and ask for more books on the subject.

● Be absolutely still and silent for five minutes and "listen" to God. God's not dead, but with all the noise in our lives God's voice is sometimes hard to hear. Consider using a Bible to help you listen.

2. Which Is Right: Evolution or Creation?

Individual Work
One Christian Perspective to Think About

To answer this question properly, we must first define our terms. What is evolution? To some, it means that all living things are constantly improving themselves. These people tend to apply this theory to all parts of life, creating more of a philosophy than a scientific theory. This philosophy causes a huge division between faith and science on the subject of creation.

What others see as evolution is simply observable fact: Many living animals can be seen to change through the generations so that variations of different species become prevalent.

The third definition of evolution, at which this question and answer are directed, states that all living things have evolved from a single source that came originally from inorganic matter.

Evolutionists and creationists come up with different answers on this question largely because of the assumptions they start with. Evolutionists start out seeking the origin of life with the assumption that God doesn't exist. Creationists assume God does exist. Because of the differing starting points, the two groups can look at the same evidence, choose which parts to rely on as most trustworthy, and draw two completely different conclusions.

So who is right? If you believe the Bible and begin with the assumption that God exists, then creation must be right (see Genesis 1:1–2:3). However, you don't have to close your eyes to scientific fact and accept creation totally by faith. Here are a few of the many scientific facts that creationists use to support their belief.

● Scientific dating methods used to date fossils depend on atmospheric conditions remaining constant since the beginning of life; that may not have been the case, especially if one believes the worldwide flood as described in the Bible.

● The laws of probability point to the existence of a creator. For even the simplest amino acid to have formed by chance, the earth would have to be at least twelve times older than scientists say it is. The fact that amino acids, the building blocks of life, exist at all indicates an intelligent creator.

● Many deposits of fossil strata do not match the geologic column supported by evolutionary theory. Supposed *older* fossils are deposited directly on top of *younger* ones, with no evidence that the strata has been flipped.

● Fossils can form only when organisms are buried so quickly that they have no time to decay or be eaten by scavengers. This fact seems to support the notion that a cataclysmic event—such as a worldwide flood—created the vast majority of fossils we see today.

● The fossil record provides no evidence at all of gradual changes occurring to transform one species into another.

● The Second Law of Thermodynamics states that anything which is organized tends, with time, to become disorganized. For this reason, our ordered universe could not have developed on its own from the chaos of the big bang. It must have had an ordered creator.[1]

But that's not all. One more factor plays into this question: Could God in some way have used evolution in creating the world? Some people say no—that God created the world in a literal six days, and there was no time for anything to evolve. Others believe that the "days" of creation may not have been literal days, but could have been extended periods of time, even millions of years.

People holding this view make room for God to have used evolution to create various species of living things. For you, the answer to this question depends on how literally you interpret the Bible and the seven days of creation.

Whether you believe that God created the world in six twenty-four-hour days or over many millions of years, the most important factor to grasp is that God acted in creation. The universe didn't come about simply by chance or on its own through a big bang. God created it and us and every living thing around us.

My Thoughts, Feelings, and Questions

Write your answers on the back of this paper.
- What have you believed about the beginning of the universe up to this point? Why?
- What questions do you wish God would've answered in the Bible about creation?
- Read Psalm 104. How does this Psalm make you feel?

Commit It to Memory

"He set the earth on its foundations; it can never be moved. You covered it with the deep as with a garment; the waters stood above the mountains."
—Psalm 104:5-6

QUESTIONS TO TALK ABOUT AS A GROUP

When everyone has read the Christian perspective and completed the journaling section, discuss these questions as a group.

● From what you can observe, do you believe that living things are constantly improving themselves? How would this belief affect one's understanding of creation?

● Is the notion that the earth took millions of years to form irreconcilable with the belief in God as creator? with the biblical explanation of creation? Explain.

● Read Genesis 7:17-23. How does belief in a worldwide flood affect one's view of the fossil and geological data uncovered by the scientific community?

● Can we trust the Bible to be accurate on such scientific things as the beginning of life? Explain.

● How does one's belief regarding creation and evolution affect one's faith?

● Why do you think the theory of evolution is so popular?

● If someone proved evolution was absolute fact, would you still believe in God? Why or why not?

● If someone proved creation was absolute fact, would you still believe in science? Why or why not?

SMALL-GROUP WORK

Give each student a copy of the "Faith Challenge" handout (p. 19). Ask youth to form small groups of three to five students. In their groups, have students read the challenging perspectives on the handout and discuss the questions that follow each one.

Jump-Start

If your group discussion needs a jump-start, read the following quotations and discuss the questions as a group.

"To suppose that God formed man from the dust with bodily hands is very childish...God neither formed man with bodily hands nor did he breathe upon him with throat and lips."[2]—St. Augustine

● Should the creation story be taken literally or figuratively? the book of Genesis? the Bible?
● Did God create the world in seven days or millions of years?
● Do you think the scientific community is purposely trying to disprove Christianity? Explain.
● Should science and theology be kept separate? Why or why not?

"All of creation is a song of praise to God."[3]—Hildegard of Bingen

● Do you see God's work in creation? Why or why not?
● Think about the star that is farthest from earth. Now think about what's beyond that star. Does the concept of eternity make it easier or more difficult to believe in God?
● What amazes you about creation?
● How does creation sing "a song of praise to God"?

FAITH CHALLENGE
How Should Christians Respond to the Following Argument?

Creation is a myth, as is the whole Bible. Through scientific investigation we know that humans are simply biochemical beings. Over the course of billions of years, life has evolved through biological changes from a single-celled organism to the intricate human being and all other species as well.

The following evidence supports this theory.

● All living organisms are composed of the same basic chemical substances.

● Unused organs in animals and people—for example, the appendix in humans—seem to represent "throwbacks" to an earlier stage of evolution when those organs were useful.

● The fact that mutations do occur in present-day species indicates that evolutionary change is possible. If a mutation turns out to be favorable, a whole new species may be created.

● The fossil record of the earth seems to indicate an evolutionary progression from ancient, simple organisms to more recent, complex organisms.

● Techniques used for dating fossils and rocks indicate that the earth is about five billion years old. This allows enough time for life to develop on earth according to evolutionary theory.[4]

● How would you live your life differently if you subscribed to this belief wholeheartedly?

● Do you think evolutionary theory can account for human behavior unrelated to the survival of the species, such as the love of beauty, the creation of art, and self-sacrificial acts in war? Explain.

● Read Psalm 139:13-18. What does this passage suggest is the meaning of life?

● For an evolutionist, what is the meaning of life?

● Is creation or evolution more appealing to you? Explain.

How Should Christians Respond to the Following Argument?

The theory of evolution has too many holes in it to accept as reliable for the origin of life. Creationism demands an all-powerful being who could create something out of nothing, and that is extremely unlikely. Thus, we don't really know how the universe or life came about. One possibility for the beginning of life on earth is the involvement of extraterrestrial beings (see Genesis 6:1-4). Strange, ancient formations on earth that are only recognizable from far above the earth's surface tend to support that theory.

● This perspective seems comfortable with not knowing all the details about how the universe or life came about. Are you as comfortable leaving the question of origins unanswered? Why or why not?

● What do you think Genesis 6:1-4 is talking about?

● Why do some people have such a hard time accepting "an all-powerful being who could create something out of nothing"?

● Read Hebrews 11:3. Can the question of origins be answered entirely by scientific or rational means? Why or why not?

● Where does this passage say that matter came from?

PAIR SHARE

Pair Share

Write the following questions on newsprint or a dry-erase board where everyone can see them. Ask teenagers to form pairs and discuss the questions with their partners.

- Do your classes in school present evolution as a theory or as a fact?
- Have you ever had difficulty standing up for your belief regarding the origin of life?
- How might the distinction between fact and theory affect your faith in God and your faith in science?
- Tell your partner about a lingering question or misgiving you have about the origin of life. To what extent does this affect your faith in God?
- Help each other see to what extent the questions you have challenge your faith and trust in God.

GROUP WORK

Group Work

Pray sentence prayers thanking God for an aspect of creation that you appreciate.

CLOSING

Closing

Give each student a copy of the "My Response" handout (p. 21). Encourage youth to write out their prayers in response to God, using the prayer-starter on the handout. Then point out the action plans they can do in response to what they've learned in this lesson.

After time for personal prayer, you may want to finish the lesson with a group prayer.

MY RESPONSE
Prayer

Dear God: Help me to never lose sight of you in a world that often tries to deny your existence and minimize your involvement. Help me to...

_____

_____

_____

ACTION PLANS

Try these ideas for putting what you've talked about into action.

● Use television, newspapers, and magazines to keep up-to-date on scientific discoveries that further complicate the theory of evolution. Also, be on the lookout for reports that approach evolution as a fact rather than an unproven theory.

● Thank God for all the mysteries in creation.

● Make a list of all the questions that evolution raises rather than answers.

"In the beginning God created the heavens and the earth."
—Genesis 1:1.

3. How Is Jesus Different From Mohammed and Buddha?

INDIVIDUAL WORK
Individual Work
One Christian Perspective to Think About

"Christianity may work fine for you, but it just doesn't work for me." "We'll all end up in the same place anyway." "I believe Jesus walked on earth as a great teacher, and I think he did some really important stuff to show us how to live, but what's the big deal? That doesn't mean he's God." "Who are you to tell me what to believe?" "We all believe basically the same thing anyway."

A lot of people say it doesn't matter who you follow. Jesus, Buddha, Mohammed—they were all great teachers who taught basically the same thing. They all provided pathways to God.

It seems to make sense, doesn't it? And it sounds so good. I mean, isn't it comforting to believe everyone will be in heaven someday? I know sometimes I'd like to think that telling other people about Jesus just isn't important. I'd like to avoid taking that risk of rejection.

But Jesus is important. His message was different from Buddha's and Mohammed's. His life and death were different also. When you take a close look at what all three of the leaders said and did, you realize that their ideas are contradictory and you can't choose them all.

Mohammed spent long periods of time in meditation. At age forty, he began to denounce the popular pantheistic religions of his day that taught all religions lead to God. He proclaimed to his culture that Allah was "one." He became the leader of the political/religious movement called Islam. He never claimed to be God, but he did claim that his teachings came directly from Allah. In order to be a Muslim, Mohammed's followers must live out the five pillars of Islam which include regular fasting, giving to the poor, going on a spiritual pilgrimage to Mecca, praying five times daily, and testifying that Mohammed is the prophet of the only god, Allah.

Buddha's actual name was Gautama. He was the son of a ruler in the modern country of Nepal. At age twenty-nine, he went on a pilgrimage to find the solution to the problem of suffering. Believing he had found the answer through meditation, he taught others that the way to "enlightenment," or freedom from suffering, was through focused rejection of human desires. Buddhists are taught to reach Nirvana (the ultimate state of consciousness) through meditation and good living. Buddha never claimed to be God; in fact, he rejected the importance and relevance of the existence of God.[1]

Jesus fulfilled ancient prophecies about his life, death, and resurrection. These predictions were fulfilled by only one person. No one, except Jesus, fulfilled the specific prophecies that described him hundreds, and even thousands, of years before his birth (see Luke 4:14-21 for an example).

Jesus predicted his own death and resurrection and rose from the dead. His specific foreknowledge of his death and his power over that death show that he is God, not just another great teacher or prophet (see Luke 18:31-33).

Jesus said he was God. Jesus never claimed that everyone was God or that all religions lead to the same place. Jesus said that he was *the* way and *the* truth. Again and again, he stated that he was God. If he *thought* he was the one and only true God but wasn't, then he certainly wasn't a great teacher that we should listen to. If he *knew* he wasn't God but claimed to be God anyway, then he was just a really good con man, leading hundreds of thousands of people astray over the course of thousands of years (see John 7:25-44).

Jesus' teaching was perfect. Jesus taught with authority, clarity, and certainty. No one can match his knowledge of his audience and his ability to reach the hearts of people, either drawing them to himself or making them really mad.

Jesus was not just another religious guru, out to win followers or to set an example with his life. He was and is God. He lives today because he conquered the ultimate power—death.[2]

My Thoughts, Feelings, and Questions

Write your answers on the back of this paper.
- How does it make you feel when Christianity claims that every other religion is in error?
- Read John 14:6-7. What do each of the words "way," "truth," and "life" mean to you?

Commit It to Memory

"I am the way and the truth and the life. No one comes to the Father except through me."—John 14:6

QUESTIONS TO TALK ABOUT AS A GROUP

When everyone has read the Christian perspective and completed the journaling section, discuss these questions as a group.

- What do you find admirable in Buddha's and Mohammed's world views?
- What are the major differences between Buddha, Mohammed, and Jesus that you see?
- Which explanations of Jesus' life that the author gives are most appealing to you? Why?
- Read John 10:7-9. Why might holding the Christian perspective of Jesus make you an unpopular person?
- Does the Christian perspective interfere with the idea that God is love? Why or why not?
- What problems do you see with other interpretations of Jesus' life that you've encountered?

SMALL-GROUP WORK

Give each student a copy of the "Faith Challenge" handout (p. 26). Ask youth to form small groups of three to five students. In their groups, have students read the challenging perspectives on the handout and discuss the questions that follow each one.

Jump-Start

If your group discussion needs a jump-start, read the following quotations and discuss the questions as a group.

"The spiritual Christ was infallible; Jesus, as material manhood, was not Christ."[3]—Mary Baker Eddy

- What is Eddy saying?
- Do you agree or disagree with this quote? Explain.
- Why do you think it's so hard for people to accept Jesus' divinity and uniqueness?
- If Jesus is the only way to God, does that mean that God will send entire populations who haven't heard of Christ to hell? Explain.

"For two thousand years Jesus Christ has been the one central character of human history."[4]—Anonymous

- Do you agree or disagree with this quote? Explain.
- If a person has had a major impact on human history, does their world view automatically deserve consideration? Explain.
- What would Christianity look like if you removed Jesus' claim of being God? of being the only way to God?

FAITH CHALLENGE
How Should Christians Respond to the Following Argument?

Jesus, like Mohammed and Buddha, was a highly evolved being who provides an example of what we should all strive to become. He also showed us what all of humanity can become in the future if we all realize the potential we have. Each person is divine, and Jesus' teachings can show us that when we realize and tap into our divinity, the earth will become a better place. Because Jesus reached a higher state of self-realization, we can follow his example to reach that state ourselves.

When Jesus talked about "sin," he was actually talking about the mistake of not seeing the God within us. To fix this problem, we need to change our hearts and minds, pursuing our own divinity. Jesus wasn't *the* Christ; the Christ was Jesus. In other words, there isn't just one Christ—we're all "Christs." Jesus, Buddha, Mohammed, and other great religious leaders were examples of what we all should be.[5]

- Does this perspective appeal to you? Why or why not?
- Have you ever heard someone say this? What would you say to a friend who expressed this viewpoint?
- Read 2 Corinthians 12:9-10. How is the source of power that Paul is talking about different from the source of power spoken about in the above perspective?
- Read 1 John 1:8-10. What's a real obstacle to becoming more Christlike according to this passage?

How Should Christians Respond to the Following Argument?

All the world's religions worship the same God, using different names. Islam calls God Allah; Buddhism calls him Buddha; Christianity calls him Jesus. They're all the same God, and they can all lead you to heaven if you worship them sincerely. It's the spiritual dimension to life that's important—not what church you join or religion you believe. Mohammed, Buddha, and Jesus Christ all teach the same path to a higher plane of personal development.[6]

- Do you think that Jesus, Mohammed, and Buddha teach the same things? Give examples of similarities and differences.
- What would someone who supports this argument say to the fact that Jesus, Buddha, and Mohammed taught principles that contradict each other?
- How do you account for the similarities between Islam and Christianity?
- Read Acts 4:12. What does this Scripture say about all religions leading to the same place?
- Why is it not possible for all religions to be right?
- Why do you think God cares about what your spirituality looks like or who you follow?

PAIR SHARE

Write the following questions on newsprint or a dry-erase board where everyone can see them. Ask teenagers to form pairs and discuss the questions with their partners.

- Who do your friends say Jesus is?
- How do you respond to friends who think Jesus was simply a good teacher just like all the other founders of world religions?
- Tell your partner who you think Jesus is and what that belief means for your life.

GROUP WORK

Set aside a time of prayer when people can speak aloud names of friends or family members who need to realize that Jesus is the only way to heaven.

CLOSING

Give each student a copy of the "My Response" handout (p. 28). Encourage youth to write out their prayers in response to God, using the prayer-starter on the handout. Then point out the action plans they can do in response to what they've learned in this lesson.

After time for personal prayer, you may want to finish the lesson with a group prayer.

MY RESPONSE
Prayer

Dear God: Help me to communicate to the world the importance of believing only in Jesus. I'd like to pray for (name of a person)…

_____

_____

_____

ACTION PLANS

Try these ideas for putting what you've talked about into action.

● Get a map of the world and pray for a different country every day, asking God to help the citizens of that country understand that Jesus is the only way to God.

● The next time you meet people who claim that all religions lead to the same place, ask them if they've read the religious writings of each group. Offer to read some of the literature of each religion with them so that together you can gain a better understanding about what each religion is really teaching. Start with the Bible and use it as a reference point for all your discussions.

● List all the ways that Jesus is unique and different from Buddha and Mohammed. Create a second list, giving reasons you're a Christian rather than a Buddhist or Muslim.

4. What Happened When Jesus Died on the Cross and Was Resurrected?

INDIVIDUAL WORK

One Christian Perspective to Think About

The cross. Almost every Christian church has at least one hanging or sitting somewhere in the building. People write songs about it. I have a couple of friends who have cross tattoos. Its likeness is displayed on merchandise ranging from Bible covers and album covers to T-shirts and breath mints. And in those movies you don't like to admit scare you, some priest always uses this little cross to try to take on a bunch of evil spirits, ghosts, demons, or other assorted supernatural beings with funny voices.

The empty tomb. Something you talk about on Easter, just before you dye the eggs, find the candy, and stuff yourself with ham or some other food your family has decided must be served on Easter. A hole in the side of a mountain with a big rock in front of it. And for some reason, people like to draw the tomb as if a big, bright light is shining right out the front.

So what's the big deal? What's the importance of the cross, and where is its power? It isn't an especially attractive symbol, and it's not really very cheery, either. What makes the cross the primary symbol of Christian faith and of Jesus' presence? What does it have to do with you? And why is the empty tomb so important?

These are tough questions. Fortunately, God's Word has answers.

Because everyone is sinful, nobody can be in a relationship with God on his or her own. In fact, because we don't measure up to God's standard of perfection, we all deserve to die and be separated from God forever.

But because God loves us and wants us to spend forever in heaven with him, he sent his Son. Jesus lived here for just over thirty years to show us what God is like, then died a cruel and painful death at the hands of the people he loved (see John 19).

But Christ's death was actually a part of God's plan. It was the culmination of thousands of years of showing love to people. When Jesus died on the cross, he was dying in our place. He took our sin on himself, as if he had done all that bad stuff instead of us. Since we deserved punishment for our sin, he took the punishment himself. So if we choose to accept his death in our place and acknowledge him as our Savior, we don't get that punishment (see Romans 3:21-26). When God sees us, he sees that our sin has already been paid for so we can hang out with God in heaven forever.

But hey! It doesn't stop there! If Jesus had stayed in the tomb, his death wouldn't have meant anything! Death would have defeated God, ensuring that we'd all be separated from God forever.

The picture is a lot better than that. Three days after Jesus died, he came back to life (see Matthew 28:5-7)! He was seen by hundreds of witnesses and interacted with lots of people before he ascended to heaven. His resurrection shows that God has power over death and that by accepting Jesus' death in our place, we'll live forever in heaven with him.

My Thoughts, Feelings, and Questions

Write your answers on the back of this paper.

● How does it make you feel when someone willingly takes the blame for something you've done?

● Read Romans 5:6-8. Would you die for a friend? an enemy? Explain.

● What two things *would* you die for? Why?

Commit It to Memory

"But God demonstrates his own love for us in this: While we were still sinners, Christ died for us."—Romans 5:8

QUESTIONS TO TALK ABOUT AS A GROUP

When everyone has read the Christian perspective and completed the journaling section, discuss these questions as a group.

- Why do you think people say that Jesus' resurrection is the most important belief in Christianity?
- What is difficult for you to understand about the way God chose to pay for humanity's sins?
- Why do you think God instructed the Israelites to sacrifice animals to cover the sins of people? How does this relate to the sacrifice Jesus made?
- Why do you think some people have a hard time accepting this?
- Read Romans 5:9-11. Why do we need to be made right with God?
- Why do you think God wants a relationship with us so much that he would die for the opportunity?

SMALL-GROUP WORK

Give each student a copy of the "Faith Challenge" handout (p. 32). Ask youth to form small groups of three to five students. In their groups, have students read the challenging perspectives on the handout and discuss the questions that follow each one.

Jump-Start

If your group discussion needs a jump-start, read the following quotations and discuss the questions as a group.

"And if Christ has not been raised, your faith is futile; you are still in your sins."—1 Corinthians 15:17

- Why would your faith be futile if Christ hadn't been raised?
- Are there any other ways in which your faith can become futile? If so, what would it look like?
- What's so bad about being "in your sins"? Isn't that just being "real" and part of being human?
- Why do Christians continue to sin?

"The Cross does not abolish suffering, but transforms it, sanctifies it, makes it fruitful, bearable, even joyful, and finally victorious."[1]—Joseph Rickaby

- How does the cross transform suffering?
- Why didn't all pain, suffering and sin end with Jesus' death?
- What difference has Jesus' death made in your life?
- What about Jesus' death is difficult for people to understand?

FAITH CHALLENGE
How Should Christians Respond to the Following Argument?

Jesus died to show humans what it means to give your life for others. He wasn't taking our place in death. He was just showing an example of self-sacrifice and selfless love. After Jesus died, he was resurrected in a figurative sense in the hearts of his friends. Because of their love for him and their faith in him, they saw him as alive, even though he was still dead.

- Who is Jesus according to this viewpoint?
- How would Christianity be different if Jesus didn't literally rise from the dead?
- Read Acts 10:39-43. Why do you think God didn't allow everyone to see Jesus?
- Why did God allow so many to see Jesus?
- Of all the things that Peter and the disciples must have done with the resurrected Christ, why did he mention eating and drinking?
- Jesus' disciples were later put to death for their faith in him. If you were one of them and you knew that he really didn't rise from the dead, would you die for that belief? Explain.

How Should Christians Respond to the Following Argument?

Jesus never really died. While he was on the cross, he passed out from the pain and stress of his condition. Everybody thought he was dead, so they took him off the cross, wrapped him in burial cloths, and put him in the tomb. Later, in the cool, damp air of the tomb, he woke up and pushed the stone aside. He walked out and appeared to his followers.

- Is this believable? Why or why not?
- Read Matthew 27:57–28:15. According to this Scripture, what are some problems with this theory?
- Why were some people interested in keeping Jesus' resurrection a secret?
- In what ways do we intentionally, or unintentionally, keep his resurrection a secret?
- What are some ways you can announce the good news of Jesus' resurrection?

PAIR SHARE

Write the following questions on newsprint or a dry-erase board where everyone can see them. Ask teenagers to form pairs and discuss the questions with their partners.

- How does it make you feel knowing that a blameless man willingly died for you?
- What do Jesus' death and resurrection mean in your life?
- Tell your partner about areas in your life that need to be made right before God, or forgiven, through Jesus. In the spirit of Christ, show each other understanding and love in spite of these shortcomings.

GROUP WORK

Commit to pray for your partner daily for the next week. As a reminder, write on a separate sheet of paper how you will specifically pray for your partner so that he or she might grow in Christ.

CLOSING

Give each student a copy of the "My Response" handout (p. 34). Encourage youth to write out their prayers in response to God, using the prayer-starter on the handout. Then point out the action plans they can do in response to what they've learned in this lesson.

After time for personal prayer, you may want to finish the lesson with a group prayer.

MY RESPONSE
Prayer

Dear God: Help me to fully grasp the extent of my sin and my need of your forgiveness and grace. Help me to...

_____

_____

_____

ACTION PLANS

Try these ideas for putting what you've talked about into action.

● Read Josh McDowell's book *Evidence That Demands a Verdict* for a deeper understanding of the central importance of Jesus' resurrection.

● Tell someone this week about the importance of Jesus' resurrection.

● Keep a daily journal listing the ways you're grateful for Jesus' sacrifice for you.

● Plan a fun outreach activity such as attending a Christian concert or watching and discussing a movie that deals with the theme of reconciliation. Invite your friends to come hear about the meaning of Jesus' death and resurrection.

5. What Is Salvation All About?

INDIVIDUAL WORK
One Christian Perspective to Think About

"Salvation" is one of those words that no one seems to agree about. Television preachers say that God will save us from our sins, while New Age philosophers teach that true salvation comes from recognizing the "god" that is within each of us.

The Bible says a great deal about salvation. In fact, the Bible uses the words "salvation" and "save" more than four hundred times. When the Bible talks about salvation, it often focuses on what God has done for us in the past, what he does for us in the present, or what he will do for us in the future.

If we accept Christ's death for our sins, God forgives all our sins—past, present, and future. The Bible clearly teaches that everyone has sinned and that the penalty for sin is death—eternal separation from God (see Romans 3:23 and 6:23). The good news of salvation, however, is that God removes the penalty of our sin. Although we *are* guilty, God declares us innocent. God forgives our death sentence because Christ already died in our place on the cross (see Romans 4:23-25 and 5:6-8). As a result of Christ's saving death, we are no longer enemies of God. Rather, we're God's friends, fully accepted sons and daughters in God's family (see Romans 5:1-2, 9-11).

In addition to forgiving our sins, God gives us the Holy Spirit to help us live as we should. The Holy Spirit makes us spiritually alive, which enables us to overcome the power of sin in our lives. The Holy Spirit breaks the power of sin so we're able to reject our sinful impulses and desires (see Romans 8:9-10). The Holy Spirit helps us grow closer to God by giving us the power to overcome the sin within us (see Galatians 5:16).

God promises that we'll live forever in heaven with him. Sin and death were never a part of God's plan for humanity. We're responsible for both. But God loves us so much that he promises to overcome our evil with his good. So because of what Jesus did for us on the cross, God will take those of us who trust in Jesus to live with him in heaven. There we will enjoy a perfect physical and spiritual existence. God will give us new and perfect bodies that never experience pain, sickness, or suffering (see Isaiah 25:8). God will also remove every trace of sin so we can live in perfect harmony with God, other Christians, and every part of God's new creation (see 1 Corinthians 15:42-57). In heaven, everything and everyone will be just as God planned from the beginning, and we will all live in perfect peace and contentment forever.

My Thoughts, Feelings, and Questions

Write your answers on the back of this paper.
- What do you need to be saved from personally?
- Read Romans 6:23. What about eternal life are you most looking forward to?

Commit It to Memory

"For the wages of sin is death, but the gift of God is eternal life in Christ Jesus our Lord."—Romans 6:23

QUESTIONS TO TALK ABOUT AS A GROUP

When everyone has read the Christian perspective and completed the journaling section, discuss these questions as a group.

- What is salvation to you?
- Read Romans 8:1-4. How could you make up for your sins if Jesus didn't pay the price for you?
- How would you try to make up for them?
- What do you think we need to do to receive salvation from God?
- Why is it so important for salvation to be a free gift?
- Do you think it's possible to lose your salvation? Why or why not?
- How would you explain salvation to a friend who didn't understand it?
- What is your idea of living in perfect harmony with God, humanity, and creation?
- How does salvation have an impact on our lives *before* we die?

SMALL-GROUP WORK

Give each student a copy of the "Faith Challenge" handout (p. 38). Ask youth to form small groups of three to five students. In their groups, have students read the challenging perspectives on the handout and discuss the questions that follow each one.

Jump-Start

If your group discussion needs a jump-start, read the following quotation and discuss the questions as a group.

"The Church is like an ark of Noah, outside of which nobody can be saved."[1]—St. Thomas Aquinas

- Does church attendance automatically guarantee salvation? Explain.
- What part does the local church play in our salvation?
- How do we become a part of Christ's Body, the Church?
- Is there a way to be absolutely certain of your salvation? Explain.

FAITH CHALLENGE
How Should Christians Respond to the Following Argument?

The road to salvation begins with confessing that "there is no god but Allah and…Mohammed is the Messenger of Allah." On this foundation, called the *shahada,* rests the other four duties required of all Muslims. In addition to confessing the *shahada,* one must offer prayers or worship—*salat*—five times each day, generally while facing Mecca, the holy city of Islam. The third pillar of Islam is *zakat,* the giving of 2.5 percent of one's income and property to the poor. Salvation also requires the observance of *sawm.* During the month of Ramadan, one must avoid all food, drink, and sexual activity during daylight hours. Finally, the *hajj,* a pilgrimage to Mecca, must be done by anyone who is able at least once in a lifetime. Those who fulfill these five requirements will receive salvation from Allah, the only true God.[2]

- What do you like and dislike about this perspective?
- Are there any duties that are required of Christians for salvation? If so, what are they?
- Read Ephesians 2:4-9. How does this Scripture refute this argument?
- Do good works have a place in Christianity? Explain.

How Should Christians Respond to the Following Argument?

The problems of this world are real, but they can't be overcome or solved. They can only be escaped. We experience problems such as sickness, hunger, pain, and poverty when we allow ourselves to be trapped in the physical world, when we focus on our physical problems instead of our spiritual potential. Within each one of us is a divine spark that needs to be set free to experience the fullness of salvation. By recognizing the god potential within us, we're able to save ourselves from all the problems and evils of this physical world. Salvation is within us. We simply need to gain the knowledge of ourselves and of the higher world that will save us and set us free from the constraints of our physical world.

- What about this perspective appeals to you? What about it doesn't make sense?
- Do you believe that problems in this world can't be solved? Explain.
- Is this argument consistent with what you know about human nature? Explain.
- Read Romans 3:10-18. Do you agree wholeheartedly with this quote that Paul uses? Why or why not?
- How would you respond to a friend who believed that there was a god within us all?

PAIR SHARE

Write the following questions on newsprint or a dry-erase board where everyone can see them. Ask teenagers to form pairs and discuss the questions with their partners.

- With regard to the Christian perspective of salvation, what do you find difficult to come to terms with?
- Personally, how do you know that God has saved you?
- Tell your partner about something you need God's help to overcome.

GROUP WORK

Have a minute or two of silence during which everyone can pray for three individuals who need a better understanding of God's salvation.

CLOSING

Give each student a copy of the "My Response" handout (p. 40). Encourage youth to write out their prayers in response to God, using the prayer-starter on the handout. Then point out the action plans they can do in response to what they've learned in this lesson.

After time for personal prayer, you may want to finish the lesson with a group prayer.

My Response
Cf My Response
Prayer

Dear God: You are my eternal hope and only salvation. Thank you for…

_____

_____

_____

Action Plans

Try these ideas for putting what you've talked about into action.

● Read the verses listed in "One Christian Perspective to Think About." Then pray and ask God to reveal people in your life who need salvation. Try to pray for them regularly.

● Ask God to reveal the areas of your life that need the redeeming touch of the Holy Spirit.

● Create or buy a symbol to represent Christ's salvation, such as a cross. Every time you see it or touch it, remember Jesus' sacrifice and offer a prayer of thanks.

● Set up a trust fall. Have six people form two lines standing face to face, three on each side. Have them hold their arms away from their chests and then reach out with both arms to grab the forearms of the person in front of them to form a "safety web." Then have a seventh person stand at the end of the line on a chair facing away from the group, fold his or her arms, and fall backward into the group's arms while keeping his or her back straight and eyes closed. Give everyone a chance to fall, and then discuss how it felt to blindly trust your friends to catch you and how this is like and unlike trusting God for salvation.

"Three things are necessary for the salvation of man: to know what he ought to believe; to know what he ought to desire; and to know what he ought to do."[3]

—St. Thomas Aquinas

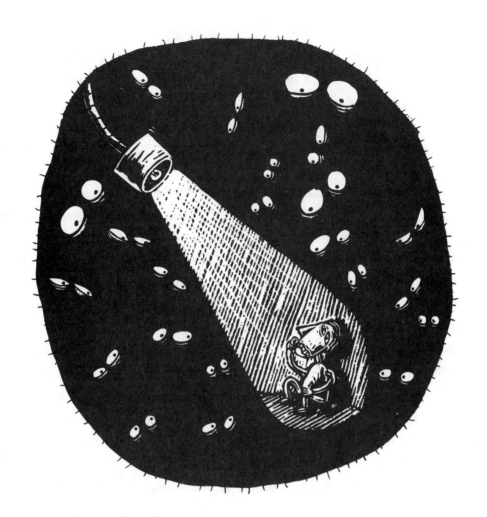

6. Will God Forgive Any and Every Sin?

INDIVIDUAL WORK
One Christian Perspective to Think About

When I was about nine years old, I lived in mortal fear of committing the one sin for which God would send me to hell. Although I was a Christian and believed that Christ had paid the penalty for sin on the cross, I thought that God simply wouldn't forgive me if I committed this one terrible sin.

I'm not the only person who has struggled with this. Many people believe that God won't forgive them if they have sex before marriage, commit suicide, curse God, or blaspheme the Holy Spirit.

The Bible teaches that Christ died on the cross to pay the penalty for all our sins (see 2 Corinthians 5:14 and 1 Peter 3:18), but it also states that some people won't be forgiven, that they'll be punished for their sins (see Matthew 25:31-43). To resolve this apparent contradiction, we need to understand several key biblical ideas.

God offers to forgive every person and every sin. God never planned for sin to be part of our world. However, when Adam and Eve disobeyed God, sin became an inescapable part of our makeup and reality (see Romans 5:12). Since God is holy, he couldn't act as though our sins didn't exist—not even the "small" ones. He had to punish them. But God also loves us, so he provided a way to forgive our sins without violating his holy nature. That is, God punished Jesus for our sins so we could receive the forgiveness that we all need (see Romans 5:6-8). God offers this forgiveness to every person who will accept it. Moreover, God offers to forgive any and every sin we commit.

Jesus taught that one sin will not be forgiven. Although God offers to forgive every sin, there is one sin that will not be forgiven (see Matthew 12:22-32; Mark 3:20-30). During Jesus' time on earth, the Holy Spirit enabled Jesus to perform many miracles to prove that he was Israel's Messiah and God's Son. However, some of the people who saw these miracles attributed them to the power of Satan rather than the power of the Holy Spirit. They rejected the Spirit's proof that Jesus had been sent by God. By doing this, they blasphemed the Holy Spirit. Jesus declared that this one sin—rejecting the Holy Spirit's prompting to believe in Jesus—would not be forgiven (for more on this, see Mark 3:20-30).

"Blasphemy against the Spirit evidently is not just a one-time offense; rather, it is an ongoing attitude of rebellion—a stubborn way of life that continually resists, rejects, and insults the Holy Spirit."[1] The Pharisees Jesus reprimanded were approaching this kind of hard-hearted rejection.

My Thoughts, Feelings, and Questions

Write your answers on the back of this paper.
● Have you ever done something that felt "unforgivable"?
● Read 1 John 1:8-10. What's the one and only thing God requires from us in order to be forgiven? Do you have sins to confess to God?

Commit It to Memory

"If we confess our sins, he is faithful and just and will forgive us our sins and purify us from all unrighteousness."—1 John 1:9

QUESTIONS TO TALK ABOUT AS A GROUP

When everyone has read the Christian perspective and completed the journaling section, discuss these questions as a group.

- In your experience, what have you heard were the "unforgivable sins"?
- Will God forgive sins that we neglect or forget to repent of?
- Do you think God will forgive us if we keep committing the same sin? Why or why not?
- Since Jesus already paid for everyone's sins, why doesn't God forgive people who reject Jesus?
- Read Matthew 18:21-35. What does this passage say about God's forgiveness?
- What do you think it means to "forgive your brother from your heart"?
- In your experience, how do you bring yourself to forgive someone who's offended you?

SMALL-GROUP WORK

Give each student a copy of the "Faith Challenge" handout (p. 44). Ask youth to form small groups of three to five students. In their groups, have students read the challenging perspectives on the handout and discuss the questions that follow each one.

Jump-Start

If your group discussion needs a jump-start, read the following quotations and discuss the questions as a group.

"I tell you the truth, all the sins and blasphemies of men will be forgiven them. But whoever blasphemes against the Holy Spirit will never be forgiven; he is guilty of an eternal sin."—Mark 3:28-29

- How does this quote make you feel?
- Is this consistent with God's nature? Why or why not?
- How would you counsel a friend who thought that he or she had done this but was now seeking forgiveness?

"Pardon one offense, and you encourage the commission of many."[a]—Publilius Syrus

- Do you agree or disagree with this quote?
- Based on what you know about God, do you think he is for or against the death penalty?
- What's the difference between forgiveness and mercy?
- At what point would it be OK to stop showing mercy to a criminal? to stop offering forgiveness?

FAITH CHALLENGE
How Should Christians Respond to the Following Argument?

God knows I'm not perfect. But everyone makes mistakes sometimes. God isn't going to send me to hell because I sleep through church on Sunday or don't come to a full stop at a red light. That's ridiculous! And even if people do truly bad things sometimes, God's love is so big that he'll forgive them—automatically. I mean, it's not as if the bad things I might do are a surprise to him. He is God, right? So why would he create me, knowing I would "sin," just so he could destroy me? That just doesn't make sense. Sending people to hell (if there even is a hell) would benefit no one—not even God. But forgiving people for the mistakes they make serves everyone's best interests. It encourages people to learn from their mistakes and to change their ways, and it enables God to enjoy the love and praise of every person he created.

● Do you agree with the statement that if there were universal forgiveness and no consequences for your errors that you would learn from your mistakes? Why or why not?

● If you were never punished, would that truly serve your best interests? Explain.

● Read Revelation 4:8-11. What does God's character have to do with his stance on sin?

● Would God still be a just God if he did what the above perspective proposes? Explain.

● Read Acts 13:38-39. According to this Scripture, what's the one condition that must be met in order to be forgiven by God?

● Why do you think God puts this condition on humanity?

How Should Christians Respond to the Following Argument?

There is no sin that is unforgivable. But the choices you make while on earth affect your karma. If you make poor or evil choices, you create negative karma for yourself. If you die with negative karma, you will be reincarnated to a lower life-form. However, there will be an opportunity in your next life to ensure that your karma is good so that you will be reincarnated to a higher life-form. Eventually, you will learn enough and make the choices necessary to reach the state of eternal bliss found in Nirvana.[3]

● What about reincarnation makes sense to you? makes no sense to you?

● How do you think a Hindu who holds this perspective feels about justice? repentance?

● What does Hebrews 9:27-28 have to say about this perspective?

● What is true repentance?

● Read Luke 17:3b-4. What does Jesus say about forgiving "habitual" sinners?

● Based on Jesus' words, do you think God expects flawless behavior after repentance? Why or why not?

● What does Jesus expect from us after we commit a sin?

Pair Share

Write the following questions on newsprint or a dry-erase board where everyone can see them. Ask teenagers to form pairs and discuss the questions with their partners.

- Read Colossians 3:13. Who are some of the people you need to forgive?
- What are some of the obstacles you face when asking for forgiveness? when trying to forgive others?
- Tell your partner about a time in your life when you doubted God's forgiveness and how you overcame those doubts.

Group Work

Read James 5:16 as a group. Then find a partner and confess one sin with which you struggle. Pray for each other asking God for strength to overcome those particular weaknesses. Continue to pray for your partner throughout the next week.

Closing

Give each student a copy of the "My Response" handout (p. 46). Encourage youth to write out their prayers in response to God, using the prayer-starter on the handout. Then point out the action plans they can do in response to what they've learned in this lesson.

After time for personal prayer, you may want to finish the lesson with a group prayer.

My Response
Prayer

Dear God: Thank you for offering me forgiveness for my sins through Jesus. I accept that forgiveness and please forgive me for…

_____

_____

_____

Action Plans

Try these ideas for putting what you've talked about into action.

● Think of a person that has offended or hurt you. Since God has forgiven us, ask him to give you the strength to extend forgiveness to the person who offended you.

● Ask a person that you've offended for forgiveness.

● On small sheets of paper, have everyone write down the sins for which they feel guilty and want forgiveness. Then read Psalm 103. Get a wastebasket, and invite each person to come forward to shred their pieces of paper into tiny pieces to represent God's forgiveness. Sing or play in the background a song of forgiveness, such as "Create in Me a Clean Heart."

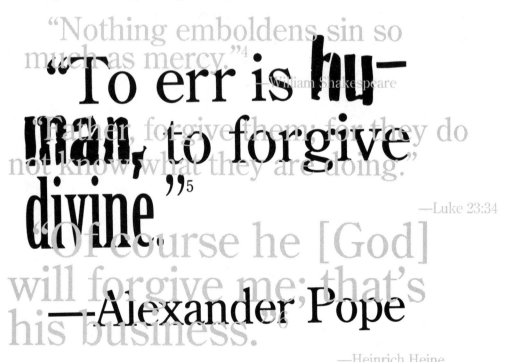

"Nothing emboldens sin so much as mercy."[4]
—William Shakespeare

"Father, forgive them; for they do not know what they are doing."
—Luke 23:34

"To err is human, to forgive divine."[5]
—Alexander Pope

"Of course he [God] will forgive me; that's his business."[6]
—Heinrich Heine

7. Why Would a Loving God Send People to Hell?

INDIVIDUAL WORK
One Christian Perspective to Think About

For starters, God does *not* send people to hell—they choose it. In fact, God has lovingly provided the only way people can avoid hell, and that is by trusting in Jesus and his death on the cross. Jesus said that he didn't come into the world to condemn the world, but that the world might be saved through him (see John 3:17). Without Jesus, every person in the world would go to hell because of choices he or she has made.

God reveals himself to people in three ways: through creation, through conscience, and through Jesus. Even though not everyone has had exposure to Jesus, every person since the beginning of time has seen God's creation and felt the uneasiness of going against one's conscience.

The Bible is quite clear: People who have lived in God's creation have seen enough of him to be moved to seek him if they wanted to. God promises to reveal himself to anyone who seeks him. So all of us are without excuse (see Romans 1:19-20).

God has also given each person a conscience—something inside of us that warns us about what's right and what's wrong (see Romans 2:15-16). However, if we ignore or suppress that little voice, eventually we'll become hardened; and it may even seem to stop warning us. Yet, because it's our choice not to obey our conscience, we are responsible for every wrong thing we do.

God's revelation to us through Jesus is the ultimate communication from God to humans. People who hear about Jesus and what he has done and choose not to respond in faith are rejecting God's love and choosing the destination of hell.

God's holiness allows no other option. It would be nice to be able to base our opinions on what we think God ought to be like. But if we fail to base our opinions on what the Bible actually teaches about God, we'll come up with ideas that have no basis in fact. A common misconception about God is that his loving nature would not allow him to condemn anyone to eternal punishment. However, that idea is not biblical. It contradicts God's perfect justice, holiness, and wisdom.

Loving a child doesn't prevent a father from allowing the child to face the consequences of his or her actions. With God the consequences of sin are severe because—as the Bible tells us—God is holy. God is by nature so pure and holy that he cannot allow people into heaven who are less than holy (see Exodus 34:6-7). By doing so, he would negate his own perfection and holiness. He would be untrue to himself and would then become imperfect.

As stated earlier, without Jesus all of us are bound for hell. Hell is separation from God—the absence of all that is good. Rejecting God results in the ultimate expression of his absence. Our only hope is to place our trust in Jesus. When he died on the cross, he paid the penalty for our sins. All we have to do is to accept the gift of eternal life he offers, and we'll be bound for eternity in heaven with him.

These conditions raise the question, "Doesn't God care if we go to hell?" Of course he does. God created every person who has ever lived on this earth, and the Bible says that he loves every one of us. He is grieved when anyone rejects him (see Psalm 78:36-40), and doesn't want anyone to end up in hell (see 2 Peter 3:9). However, God also doesn't force people to love him—God lets people choose heaven or hell through their responses to him. God cares so much that he doesn't base our entrance into heaven on what we've done. If he did that, no one would make it to heaven. Instead,

God does all the work; we simply have to acknowledge our need for the sacrifice and righteousness of Jesus Christ.

My Thoughts, Feelings, and Questions

Write your answers on the back of this paper.

● How does it make you feel to know that some of your friends, family, or acquaintances will spend eternity in hell if they don't believe in Jesus?

● Read John 3:36. Based on what you know about God, describe what eternal separation from God and all that is good would be like.

Commit It to Memory

"Whoever believes in the Son has eternal life, but whoever rejects the Son will not see life, for God's wrath remains on him."—John 3:36

QUESTIONS TO TALK ABOUT AS A GROUP

When everyone has read the Christian perspective and completed the journaling section, discuss these questions as a group.

- Do you think hell is real? Why or why not?
- Why do you think many people won't accept the fact that God will allow people to go to hell?
- How do God's love and holiness relate to heaven and hell?
- Does love mean the absence of punishment? Explain.
- How do you think God speaks to humanity through creation?
- Read 1 John 5:11-12. Do you think those people who have never heard of Jesus will go to hell? Explain.
- How were people saved before Jesus' death and resurrection (see Hebrews 11)?
- Do you think God's voice in creation and conscience is loud and clear enough to save people from hell? Why or why not?
- If each individual person chooses his or her eternal destiny, what must we do to choose heaven?

SMALL-GROUP WORK

Give each student a copy of the "Faith Challenge" handout (p. 51). Ask youth to form small groups of three to five students. In their groups, have students read the challenging perspectives on the handout and discuss the questions that follow each one.

Jump-Start

If your group discussion needs a jump-start, read the following quotation and discuss the questions as a group.

"Most people outside of Christ dismiss the concept of hell. For them, the thought of endless and infinite misery so paralyzes their minds that they refuse to think about it."[1]—D. James Kennedy

- Do you think this is really the reason people dismiss the concept of hell? Explain.
- What are some other reasons people give for not believing in hell?
- What boggles your mind when you think about eternity and the afterlife?

FAITH CHALLENGE
How Should Christians Respond to the Following Argument?

People are born basically good. Thus, there is no need for salvation. Anyone who lives life as a fairly nice person will make it to heaven. Only those who are guilty of terrible things like murder will be banished from heaven. And even then, there may be no hell for them—they may just cease to exist after they die. The Christian idea of hell was created by over-zealous monks who wanted to scare people into believing the way they did. We need to stop worrying about the afterlife and concentrate on being kind to others. After all, we're going to spend an eternity of interconnection.

● If this perspective were true, how could you tell the difference between terrible sins and sins that are dismissed by God?

● How do people who hold this viewpoint back up their statements?

● What problems do you see with this perspective?

● What do Romans 3:10-20 and Hebrews 12:14 have to say about this perspective?

PAIR SHARE

Write the following questions on newsprint or a dry-erase board where everyone can see them. Ask teenagers to form pairs and discuss the questions with their partners.

● How have you heard God's voice through his creation?

● Describe how God speaks to you through your conscience.

● As a pair, list ways by which you can become more closely tuned to God's voice through creation, conscience, and God's Word.

GROUP WORK

During prayer, allow time for people to say the names of people they know who need to put their faith in Jesus.

CLOSING

Give each student a copy of the "My Response" handout (p. 53). Encourage youth to write out their prayers in response to God, using the prayer-starter on the handout. Then point out the action plans they can do in response to what they've learned in this lesson.

After time for personal prayer, you may want to finish the lesson with a group prayer.

MY RESPONSE
Prayer

Dear God: Thank you for making it possible for us to spend eternity with you. Help (list people who need to believe in Jesus) to know you.

_____

_____

_____

ACTION PLANS

Try these ideas for putting what you've talked about into action.

● Satan wants to drag as many people to hell with him as possible. How do you think Satan is scheming to trip you up in your walk with God? Pretend to be a "senior demon" writing a short letter to a subordinate with advice about how best to get you to fall. What weaknesses would they target?

● Talk to some parents about why they think it's necessary to punish their children, even though they love them.

● Pray every day for one person who doesn't believe God allows people to go to hell. Pray that God would open the person's eyes to his or her need for Jesus.

● Give others a chance to share about a time in their lives when they realized that they fell short of God's standards and that without faith in Jesus, they would be going to hell.

"The Lord casts no one down to hell, *but the spirit casts himself thither."[2]*

— *Emanuel Swedenborg*

B. Why Does God Allow Suffering?

INDIVIDUAL WORK
One Christian Perspective to Think About

I knew a young man who was sexually abused when he was a teenager. He was later given the frightening news that the person who abused him was infected with the AIDS virus. You can imagine the anxiety and fear he faced as he waited for the results of his blood test. I remember when he asked me if *I* would still have sex with my wife if I found out I was HIV-positive. My heart sank because I knew he thought that he probably was.

What could I tell him? "If you live long enough to get married, you'll just have to forget about sex. I know the rest of the few years you have left have been changed forever; but God loves you, and it will all work out for the best." I didn't know what to say, and I didn't have the courage to tell him God loves him. "He's got a funny way of showing it!" kept playing through my head.

I couldn't and can't understand why God would let this happen to anyone. Why would God allow this young man to be robbed of his future by a twisted event? God is all-powerful (omnipotent) and all-knowing (omniscient) so we know that nothing happens on this earth without God allowing it to take place. I don't think God condoned the event that the young man suffered through, and I'm certain he didn't cause it. So I'm left with three possible reasons that God let this happen. I don't know which reason is *the* reason; it could be any combination of the three.

God allows us to choose. God gives us the opportunity to choose things that are according to his will or against it (see Deuteronomy 30:11-20). God has placed such a high value on that freedom, that he allows us to make poor choices—even if they hurt ourselves or others. When we choose poorly or even viciously, we and others must face the consequences of those choices. It's not fair that the perpetrator made the choice he did, and it's not fair that the young man must endure the consequences. The perpetrator made a horrible choice that was against God's law. A choice that led to emotional and physical suffering. God allowed him to choose, just as God allows us to choose because God values freedom.

Sin poisoned the world. After God created the world, he "saw all that he had made, and it was very good" (Genesis 1:31). Suffering was *not* a part of God's perfect creation. It entered in when Adam and Eve chose to sin against God (see Genesis 3). All of creation feels the effects of that choice (see Romans 8:18-23). Since the world is poisoned by sin, we suffer disease, pain, brokenness, genetic disorders, violence, hate, and death. The world has been poisoned by sin, and suffering is one of the horrible symptoms.

God has a bigger perspective. Sometimes God allows us to suffer for our own benefit. Think back to one of the most difficult times in your life. Can you see any good that has come out of it? Are you a different person because of it? Can you see a way in which God brought a good thing out of your difficult circumstances? Maybe he used a bad thing to shape your character and to help you grow. I can't understand the suffering that others go through, but when I look back on my life, I can see at least small ways that my own suffering had an important part in shaping who I am.

So did God allow that young man to get molested for his own good? My immediate response is "of course not." But I believe that God will bring some good out of the circumstances. Maybe the young man will extend forgiveness to the person who sinned against him. Maybe the perpetrator will turn to God for help and mercy when he's forgiven by the young man. Maybe God will use this situation to empower the young man to minister to people who have undergone similar circumstances. I don't know, but God knows. As Billy Graham says in his book *Till Armageddon,* "We humans view life from our personal point of time and space, but God views us from his heavenly throne in the light of eternity."

By the way, the young man's blood test came back negative. I know that all stories of suffering don't have happy endings, but this one might.

My Thoughts, Feelings, and Questions

Write your answers on the back of this paper.

● How does knowing that God allows suffering in the world make you feel about God?

● Read 1 Peter 5:6-11. What do you think about Peter's words of consolation to suffering Christians?

● Would these words comfort you in times of suffering? Why or why not?

Commit It to Memory

"And we know that in all things God works for the good of those who love him, who have been called according to his purpose."—Romans 8:28

QUESTIONS TO TALK ABOUT AS A GROUP

When everyone has read the Christian perspective and completed the journaling section, discuss these questions as a group.

- Is this Christian perspective consistent with what you know about God? Why or why not?
- What holes do you see in this perspective?
- What part do you think Satan has in the suffering of the world?
- Do you think Satan has free reign on earth? Explain.
- Do you think God is fair? Why or why not?
- Read Psalm 34. What verses do you think would comfort a suffering Christian and why?
- How and why does suffering draw some people closer to God? Why does suffering push some people away from God?
- Has suffering ever been a part of God's plan in your life? Explain.
- How has God been present with you or your family during a time of suffering?

SMALL-GROUP WORK

Give each student a copy of the "Faith Challenge" handout (p. 58). Ask youth to form small groups of three to five students. In their groups, have students read the challenging perspectives on the handout and discuss the questions that follow each one.

Jump-Start

If your group discussion needs a jump-start, read the following quotations and discuss the questions as a group.

"Man is sometimes extraordinarily, passionately, in love with suffering."[1]—Fyodor Dostoyevsky

- Do you agree with this quote?
- Why would someone be in love with suffering?
- Do we ever cause our own suffering? Explain.
- How has suffering had a positive impact on your life? a negative impact?

"God whispers to us in our pleasures, speaks in our conscience, but shouts in our pains: It is his megaphone to rouse a deaf world."[2]—C.S. Lewis

- What is Lewis saying?
- How does Lewis' claim that God uses suffering to get our attention make you feel about God? Explain.
- How is Lewis' idea about God consistent with your understanding of God's nature? How is it different?
- Do you think God has been successful in his attempts to "rouse a deaf world"? Why or why not?
- Do you agree that this is what God is after in allowing suffering? Explain.

FAITH CHALLENGE
How Should Christians Respond to the Following Argument?

The primary goal of existence is survival. Suffering is random and without meaning. Feelings of emotional suffering are an alarm designed to direct us away from destruction. Emotional suffering is a response to perceived or real threats to our survival and dominance. Triumph through suffering provides the opportunity to proliferate the human species thus promoting survival for the future.

- On what points does this perspective agree with Christianity?
- Where does this perspective diverge from Christianity?
- What are some of the underlying presuppositions of this perspective that are not Christian?
- Read John 16:20-24, 33. What words of Jesus do you think gave the disciples hope?
- Does suffering have meaning for a Christian? for a non-Christian?

How Should Christians Respond to the Following Argument?

Pain is a necessary part of being human. "The human life cycle of birth, development, decline, and death includes much pain and loss that are unavoidable."[3] If we truly understand the purpose and permanence of pain, we can come to understand that painful experiences provide the opportunity for new meaning and purpose.

Dukkha is an important term in Buddhist teaching. It's the word in the Sanskrit that describes the condition of human life. It's often translated into English as "suffering," but it is more like the words "dissatisfaction" or "discontent." If we misunderstand the pain we face and observe, *dukkha* interferes with our well-being and understanding. *Dukkha* can be eased and transformed into peace and joy as we confront pain and suffering, increase in awareness of our dependence and interconnection with all beings, and learn to be compassionate and tolerant.[4]

- On what points does this perspective agree with Christianity?
- Where does this perspective diverge from Christianity?
- What are some of the underlying presuppositions of this perspective that are not Christian?
- Read Isaiah 41:10. How is a Buddhist's source of strength different from a Christian's?

PAIR SHARE

Write the following questions on newsprint or a dry-erase board where everyone can see them. Ask teenagers to form pairs and discuss the questions with their partners.

- Why do you think God doesn't always let us see the way he brings good out of our circumstances?
- How would you comfort a Christian friend who was suffering? a non-Christian friend?
- Tell your partner about a time your faith was tested because of the suffering you witnessed in your family, school, or the world. How did you reconcile the suffering you saw with your faith?

GROUP WORK

As a group, pray sentence prayers for suffering individuals and groups in the world (both locally and internationally), asking God to relieve their suffering and be their comfort and hope. If your group has a hard time thinking of people or groups outside of your country, bring in a newspaper or news magazine to help stimulate prayer for the entire world.

CLOSING

Give each student a copy of the "My Response" handout (p. 60). Encourage youth to write out their prayers in response to God, using the prayer-starter on the handout. Then point out the action plans they can do in response to what they've learned in this lesson.

After time for personal prayer, you may want to finish the lesson with a group prayer.

MY RESPONSE
Prayer

Dear God: Sometimes I find it hard to trust in you when I suffer. Forgive me and…

_____

_____

_____

ACTION PLANS

Try these ideas for putting what you've talked about into action.

● If you want to learn more about suffering, read James Dobson's book *When God Doesn't Make Sense* (Tyndale House Publishers, 1993) or read Billy Graham's book *Till Armageddon* (Word Books, 1981).

● Pray for other believers around the world once a day, especially those who are suffering or are being persecuted. The prayer guide *Operation World* (Zondervan Publishing House, updated annually) is a book that gives you specific needs to pray for in each country of the world.

● Do a thematic character study of suffering individuals in the Bible to see how they responded in their individual circumstances. Some ideas are Peter (Luke 22:31-34; 54-62), Paul (the book of Acts and 2 Corinthians 12:7-10), Job (the book of Job), and Jesus (Luke 22:1-6; Mark 14:32-42).

● Make a list of people that you know who are going through difficult times; perhaps people who attend your church or school. Commit to praying for them every day for a week. Update the list the following week. Begin by praying with a partner before the close of this session. Remember to respect the privacy of others if they desire to remain anonymous.

"Nine-tenths of our suffering is caused by others
not **thinking so much of us as we
think they ought.**"[5]

—Mary Lyon

q.Who Is the Holy Spirit?

INDIVIDUAL WORK
One Christian Perspective to Think About

I know it sounds a little weird. Holy Spirit. Holy Ghost. What or who is the Holy Spirit? Where does he come from? And why does the mention of his name cause so much controversy among Christians?

In many Christian churches, the Holy Spirit is little more than a term tacked on at the end of "the Father, the Son and the..." In other churches, we focus on the Holy Spirit more than almost anything else.

The Holy Spirit can be somewhat mysterious. But we do know some things. For example, we know that the Holy Spirit is a person. Jesus referred to the Holy Spirit as "he" (John 14:15-31), and the Bible describes the Holy Spirit as *doing* things such as speaking (Revelation 2:7), testifying (John 15:26), leading (Acts 8:29), commanding (Acts 16:6-7), guiding (John 16:13), appointing (Acts 20:28), being lied to (Acts 5:3-4), being insulted (Hebrews 10:29), and being grieved (Ephesians 4:30). The Holy Spirit is not just any person, though—he's God. The Holy Spirit is eternal (Hebrews 9:14), he's everywhere at once (Psalm 139:7-10), he knows everything (1 Corinthians 2:10-11), and he created us (Genesis 1:2). Even though he's a person, and because he's God, we don't see him, physically touch him, smell him, or audibly hear him—although the Bible doesn't say these things can't happen.

When people trust that Jesus died in their place and let God be God in their lives, the Holy Spirit enters their hearts and sets up camp. (By the way, some Christians believe this "filling" of the Holy Spirit happens full force right from the start, while others believe it happens more gradually over time. Either way, the point is that it happens.) Here are a few ways the Holy Spirit chooses to operate in a person's life.

● The Holy Spirit helps us understand the truth of Christianity and the Bible (1 Corinthians 2:10).

● The Holy Spirit lives in our bodies (1 Corinthians 6:19).

● The Holy Spirit comforts and encourages us (Acts 9:31).

● The Holy Spirit guides us (John 16:13).

● The Holy Spirit convicts us when we disobey God (John 16:8).

● The Holy Spirit helps us follow Jesus and become more like him (Romans 15:16).

● The Holy Spirit helps us know what to say about God (1 Corinthians 2:13).

● The Holy Spirit shows us God's will (Acts 13:2).

● The Holy Spirit corrects us (Acts 16:6-7).

● The Holy Spirit gives us special abilities we can use to help others (1 Corinthians 12:1-11).

● The Holy Spirit draws us to himself (1 Corinthians 2:4-5).

● The Holy Spirit shows his presence in our lives by giving us a sign, or "fruit of the Spirit." The "fruit" is an outward sign that God is present with us. When we follow and obey the Holy Spirit, the fruit begins to appear: love, joy, peace, patience, kindness, goodness, faithfulness, gentleness, and self-control (Galatians 5:22-23).[1]

My Thoughts, Feelings, and Questions

Write your answers on the back of this paper.

● Of all the things listed above that the Holy Spirit does, what is most important to you?

● What characteristic of the Holy Spirit would you like to become more personally acquainted with and why?

● Read John 14:26. Has the Holy Spirit ever reminded you of Jesus' words? Briefly describe your experience.

Commit It to Memory

"But the Counselor, the Holy Spirit, whom the Father will send in my name, will teach you all things and will remind you of everything I have said to you."—John 14:26

QUESTIONS TO TALK ABOUT AS A GROUP

When everyone has read the Christian perspective and completed the journaling section, discuss these questions as a group.

- Have you experienced the Holy Spirit's presence in your life? If so, how?
- What evidence have you seen of the Holy Spirit's work at church, home, or school?
- What other notions of the Holy Spirit have you encountered?
- Read 1 John 4:1-6. How can you "test the spirits" in a practical way to be sure that you're hearing and following God's voice and not Satan's?
- Have you ever encountered the "spirit of falsehood" as this Scripture describes? If so, describe the encounter.

SMALL-GROUP WORK

Give each student a copy of the "Faith Challenge" handout (p. 65). Ask youth to form small groups of three to five students. In their groups, have students read the challenging perspectives on the handout and discuss the questions that follow each one.

Jump-Start

If your group discussion needs a jump-start, read the following quotations and discuss the questions as a group.

"By the power and permission of the Holy Spirit, the qualities of greatness are present. It's kind of like a lovely moonbeam. You hold it loosely, you enjoy its beauty...but you can't control it."[2]—Charles R. Swindoll

- Have you ever seen someone who seems to "control" the Spirit? If so, do you think this quote is accurate? Explain.
- What people do you really respect because of the way the Spirit works in and through them?
- What are the signs of spiritual greatness?

"'Did you receive the Holy Spirit when you believed?' They answered, 'No, we have not even heard that there is a Holy Spirit.'"—Acts 19:2b

- What do you think it means to receive the Holy Spirit?
- Can you believe in Jesus without having the Holy Spirit in you? Explain.
- Read Acts 19:1-7. Do people "receive" the Holy Spirit in this way today? in different ways?

Faith Challenge
FAITH CHALLENGE
How Should Christians Respond to the Following Argument?

What you call the Holy Spirit is actually just your own higher consciousness directing your life. Psychologists call it superego; New Agers call it cosmic consciousness. But the name doesn't matter. It's that part of your intelligence that exists on a higher plane. We typically use less than 10 percent of our brains. What do you think the rest of that gray matter is for?

The truth is we know a lot more than we think we know. As we continue to evolve and learn, eventually we'll see that the "Holy Spirit" is just an extension of our own intelligence, helping us make the right decisions in life.

● What would you say to someone who told you that the Holy Spirit is actually your own higher consciousness?

● Read 1 John 3:23-24. From where does the Spirit come according to this passage?

● Read 1 Corinthians 1:25. If people used 100 percent of their capabilities, how would they compare with God?

How Should Christians Respond to the Following Argument?

The Holy Spirit is just the Christian way of describing spirit guides. Spirit guides are strong souls, either from earth's past or from other worlds, who come to earth to help us make the right choices in life. Spirit guides are loving and truthful and committed to helping people find the true path. They typically speak to you in your inner soul, but may at times speak through a special person who has the unique ability to channel a spirit guide's presence through the body. So there is no Holy Spirit in the Christian sense. Instead, there are many holy spirits who come to help us through life.

● What would you say to someone who told you the Holy Spirit is actually a spirit guide who has come from the past to help you?

● Read John 14:15-20. In what ways does this Scripture contrast with the above perspective?

● Why do you think the world can't accept the one true Holy Spirit?

● How does it make you feel to know that the one true almighty God can dwell inside of you?

● How can you know for sure that the Spirit dwells inside you?

PAIR SHARE

Write the following questions on newsprint or a dry-erase board where everyone can see them. Ask teenagers to form pairs and discuss the questions with their partners.

- How can the Holy Spirit change your life?
- What can keep the Holy Spirit from changing your life?
- Tell your partner about an area in your life where you need the Holy Spirit's guidance. Help each other think of ways to be more sensitive to the Spirit's leading.

GROUP WORK

Pray aloud for the person on your right, asking God to help that person be sensitive to the Holy Spirit.

CLOSING

Give each student a copy of the "My Response" handout (p. 67). Encourage youth to write out their prayers in response to God, using the prayer-starter on the handout. Then point out the action plans they can do in response to what they've learned in this lesson.

After time for personal prayer, you may want to finish the lesson with a group prayer.

MY RESPONSE
Prayer

Dear God: Help me to be sensitive to the Holy Spirit in my life. Speak to me clearly when...

_____

_____

_____

_____

ACTION PLANS

Try these ideas for putting what you've talked about into action.

● For a study of the Holy Spirit, visit the worship services of several different kinds of churches in your area. Write down your feelings and perceptions after each service with regard to the Holy Spirit's place in corporate worship. For an even deeper study, interview church leaders from each church about the role of the Holy Spirit in their church. After your investigation, discuss your findings with your pastor.

● For one week, keep a daily journal noting all the ways you feel the Holy Spirit has been present, working, and speaking in your life.

● As a group read together Galatians 5:22-25. Form a circle, and have students each tell the person on their left what fruit of the Spirit they see in that person's life.

10. How Do Demons and Angels Influence My World?

INDIVIDUAL WORK
One Christian Perspective to Think About

People everywhere are talking about angel experiences. We even have TV shows and movies about angels. Unfortunately, much of the information in the media about angels is faulty. And many people today insist that their "angel" experiences are messages from God—even if those experiences don't fit with anything we know about God from the Bible.

So how do we know what's really true about how angels work in our world? We need to compare what people say today with what the Bible teaches us. John tells us to check out "the spirits" before believing them: "Dear friends, do not believe every spirit, but test the spirits to see whether they are from God, because many false prophets have gone out into the world" (1 John 4:1).

We can be sure of what we read about angels in the Bible. Take a look at several things the Bible says angels do.

- Angels guide people in times of special need. (Genesis 24:7; Acts 8:26).

- Angels minister to and protect those who hurt (1 Kings 19:3-8; Hebrews 1:14).

- Angels provide comfort and strength in times of sorrow and danger (Luke 22:39-44; Acts 27:21-25).

- Angels protect and deliver their charges from harm (Genesis 19:12-17).

- Angels are messengers and instruments of God's will (Matthew 28:1-7; Acts 10:1-8).

- Angels appear in dreams and visions to give warnings and announcements (Luke 1:2-14; Matthew 2:13-21).

- Angels execute God's judgment (Genesis 19:12-13).

- Angels protect people who take a stand for God (Daniel 6:19-22; Acts 12:6-10).

It's important to know that the Bible also gives a pretty clear picture of what demons and the Devil did and what they do today. TV and movies show "demonized" people, homes, and even toys. By looking at Scripture, we can put some of the myths to rest and develop an understanding of what we should and shouldn't be concerned with. The Bible shows that demons and the devil

- deceive people into doubting God (Genesis 3:1-5).

- are created beings, not the spirits of dead humans (Psalm 148:2-5; 2 Peter 2:4).

- tempt Christians to sin (Ephesians 2:1-3; 1 Thessalonians 3:5).

- seek to keep Christians from growing in their relationships with God (Ephesians 6:11-12).

- hinder Christians in serving God (1 Thessalonians 2:18).

- lead people away from God through deception (1 Timothy 4:1).

- encourage selfishness and jealousy among Christians (James 3:13-15).

- encourage persecution against Christians (Revelation 2:10).

Angels and demons are real spiritual beings. Angels are working at God's command and doing good things among us for the purpose of glorifying God. Demons are working under Satan's command and doing all they can to deceive people and keep them from believing the truth about Jesus Christ. They may even try to pass themselves off as true angels of God. "For Satan himself masquerades as an angel of light. It is not surprising, then, if his servants masquerade as servants of righteousness" (2 Corinthians 11:14-15).

Our biggest task related to angels and demons is to determine which are which. Fortunately the Bible gives us help on that point: "This is how you can recognize the Spirit of God: Every spirit that acknowledges that Jesus Christ has come in the flesh is from God, but every spirit that does not acknowledge Jesus is not from God" (1 John 4:2-4).

So what we need to do is be on the lookout. If we hear about angels who claim to be the spirits of people who have died, we must reject what they say as demonic—even if it sounds good. If we hear of an experience in which the angel does something according to biblical standards and the glory ends up going to God, there's a good chance that the experience was authentic. Unfortunately, many experiences are not so clear cut. Therefore, we need to be very careful what we accept, and to test questionable experiences according to the guidelines of Scripture before deciding if they are from God or from Satan.

One thing for sure: God and Satan are at work in our world through angels and demons, and we must be ready for the battle.

My Thoughts, Feelings, and Questions

Write your answers on the back of this paper.
● What scares you about the supernatural realm of demons and angels?
● What idea surprised you or caught your attention from the section above?
● Read Ephesians 6:12-13. When have you felt you've struggled against spiritual forces of evil?

Commit It to Memory

"For our struggle is not against flesh and blood, but against the rulers, against the authorities, against the powers of this dark world and against the spiritual forces of evil in the heavenly realms. Therefore put on the full armor of God, so that when the day of evil comes, you may be able to stand your ground, and after you have done everything, to stand."—Ephesians 6:12-13

QUESTIONS TO TALK ABOUT AS A GROUP

When everyone has read the Christian perspective and completed the journaling section, discuss these questions as a group.

● How do the ideas about angels and demons you see on television and in the movies differ from the biblical perspective?

● How can we know if a strange happening was just a coincidence or the working of an angel?

● Do angels and demons fight each other? Explain.

● If an angel does something for me, will I know it? Explain.

● How can we combat the influence of demons in our lives?

● Read Matthew 17:14-21. What does this Scripture say about demons?

● Do you think all sickness is caused by demons? Why or why not?

● What is our responsibility concerning angels and demons?

SMALL-GROUP WORK

Give each student a copy of the "Faith Challenge" handout (p. 72). Ask youth to form small groups of three to five students. In their groups, have students read the challenging perspectives on the handout and discuss the questions that follow each one.

Jump-Start

If your group discussion needs a jump-start, read the following quotations and discuss the questions as a group.

"There are two equal and opposite errors into which our race can fall about the devils [demons]. One is to disbelieve their existence. The other is to believe and feel an unhealthy interest in them."[1]—C.S. Lewis

● Do you believe in demons? Why or why not?
● Do you believe in angels? Why or why not?
● What do you think qualifies as an "unhealthy interest"?
● What are the dangers of an unhealthy interest in angels and demons? disbelieving the existence of angels and demons?

"Every devil has not a cloven hoof."[2]—Daniel Defoe

● What is Defoe saying?
● What examples of Satan's influence can you think of at school, or in our culture at large?
● If you were Satan, what subtle thing would you do to make a Christian like yourself fall?

FAITH CHALLENGE
How Should Christians Respond to the Following Argument?

Angels channel messages through people. Many people have their own angels with whom they develop friendships and converse with on a regular basis. Angels that exist to help us include the angel of unconditional love and freedom, the angel of illusion and reality, the angel of creative wisdom, and the angel of order and harmony. These angels are interconnected with tarot cards, astrological signs, and gods and goddesses worshipped by cultures in the past. For example, the angel of creative wisdom can be associated with the Egyptian goddess Isis, with the tarot card of the high priestess, and astrologically with the moon. Each angel can help you become more true to your holy self.[3]

● What do you think would attract someone to this point of view?

● What's wrong with playing with tarot cards and reading horoscopes simply for fun if you really don't believe them?

● Read 2 Corinthians 11:14-15. Based on this passage, do you think the people who have encounters with "angel guides" are making it all up, or are they having genuine experiences?

● Is Satan able to provide good things such as unconditional love, harmony, and creative wisdom? Explain.

How Should Christians Respond to the Following Argument?

Demons aren't really evil spirits sent from some mythical hell. They're actually troubled souls of men and women who have died without resolving their lives. Maybe they were murdered or violently killed in an accident. Or maybe they just weren't ready to leave behind the people they love. These spirits are restless and often do things that seem harmful or even evil to us. But with a little understanding, we can realize that, rather than fearing them, we should try to help them resolve their lives so they can pass on to the next plane of existence.

● Do you like this explanation of ghosts? Why or why not?

● How do *you* explain the existence of ghosts?

● What are the major differences between this perspective of ghosts and the biblical perspective of demons?

● Read 1 Timothy 4:1. What influence do you think demons have today?

PAIR SHARE

Write the following questions on newsprint or a dry-erase board where everyone can see them. Ask teenagers to form pairs and discuss the questions with their partners.

● How do you see your world affected by angels and demons?

● What are ways to guard against demonic attack?

● Tell your partner about a time you had an encounter with the supernatural, either with evil or good. Then pray and ask God to guard you through his Holy Spirit and his angels against the attacks of the Evil One.

GROUP WORK

As a group, pray the Lord's prayer aloud (Matthew 6:9-13).

CLOSING

Give each student a copy of the "My Response" handout (p. 74). Encourage youth to write out their prayers in response to God, using the prayer-starter on the handout. Then point out the action plans they can do in response to what they've learned in this lesson.

After time for personal prayer, you may want to finish the lesson with a group prayer.

MY RESPONSE
Prayer

My Response

Dear God: Grant me strength to resist the temptations of Satan and his demons. Help me when...

_____

_____

_____

ACTION PLANS

Try these ideas for putting what you've talked about into action.

● Become more aware of the media representations of Satan and his demons in popular culture. When you see them on posters, card decks, in magazines, television, video games or movies, question whether or not they're accurate. Pray for the people who get wrapped up in these representations or become fearful as a result.

● Ask several respected adults in the church what it means to "resist the devil" so that he will flee from you (James 4:7).

● Begin each day this week with a song of praise to God and consciously submit yourself and your activities to him.

● Ask members of your church to contribute anonymous essays that tell of personal angel encounters. Then during a weekly meeting, read them to the group and have the class evaluate how they compare to the biblical understanding of angels. This can also be done by obtaining videotapes of angel stories, such as the ones on television.

"Are not all ANGELS ministering spirits SENT TO SERVE THOSE WHO WILL INHERIT SALVATION?"

—*HebrEws 1:14*

11. How Was the Bible Written?

INDIVIDUAL WORK
One Christian Perspective to Think About

I'm working on my first novel. Actually, I've been at it for over four years now (kind of a slow start, I know). The hardest thing about writing a novel is trying to get the story to flow together. It has all sorts of characters, subplots, and tangents. There are so many details that an author has to keep straight for the book to work together. Writing takes a lot of focus. And a fair amount of luck.

Of course, the Bible makes most writing efforts look like child's play. That awesome book was written over a period of 1,600 years (about sixty generations). Different parts of the Bible were penned by fishermen, kings, scholars, peasants, and shepherds. More than forty people took part in writing God's message down. And although each author's perspective and personality was unique, God's Spirit worked through each writer in such a way that God's message was communicated to us exactly as God intended.

These authors weren't all from the same place either. Some of the writers penned their words in Asia, some in Africa, and some in Europe. They wrote in one of three languages—Hebrew, Aramaic, or Greek.[1]

Copies of their writings were passed down so future generations could have access to God's message. And God made sure that his original message was kept intact. There are thousands of ancient copies of the Bible that scholars have cross-checked to make sure the message hasn't been changed over time. (Some existing parts of the New Testament date back to the first century!)[2]

That may all sound incredible, but the real miracle is that when you put it all together, the Bible tells one unified story. From Genesis through Revelation, the story weaves a clear, powerful message: God loves us and invaded history to create a way for us to know him—through his Son, Jesus.

The story of the Bible continues today—through you, through me, through everyone who believes in Jesus. There could be no more vital story on earth than the one the Bible tells. There could be no more relevant truth than the one the Bible reveals. It really is the greatest story ever told. And even the way it came together is miraculous.

My Thoughts, Feelings, and Questions

Write your answers on the back of this paper.

● What impresses you most about how the Bible was written?

● Read Psalm 119:105-112. Do you share the psalmist's feeling about God's Word? Why or why not?

Commit It to Memory

"Your word is a lamp to my feet and a light for my path."—Psalm 119:105

QUESTIONS TO TALK ABOUT AS A GROUP

When everyone has read the Christian perspective and completed the journaling section, discuss these questions as a group.

- What might people find hard to believe about how the Bible was written?
- What are some common misconceptions about how the Bible was written?
- If someone were writing your life story, how would you make sure he or she got the story right?
- How do you think God made sure the Bible tells his story correctly?
- Why would God have so many people over so many generations write the Bible, instead of just having one or two people do it?
- Read Deuteronomy 8:3. How is God's Word like bread?

SMALL-GROUP WORK

Give each student a copy of the "Faith Challenge" handout (p. 78). Ask youth to form small groups of three to five students. In their groups, have students read the challenging perspectives on the handout and discuss the questions that follow each one.

Jump-Start

If your group discussion needs a jump-start, read the following quotations and discuss the questions as a group.

"Ignorance among younger Americans is so sweeping that our culture is in danger of losing its grasp of the one book in human history that any truly educated person must know intimately."[3]—Richard Ostling

- What ignorance do you see in today's culture?
- Do you agree or disagree that the Bible should definitely be a part of every educated person's core of knowledge (even non-Christians)? Why?
- Would you want the Bible to be taught in public schools if it meant that all other religious groups' holy books would get equal time and consideration? Explain.
- What contributions to human history has the Bible made that you think people should know about?

"It was said of one zealous apostle of free thought...that he would believe anything, so long as it was not in the Bible.'"[4]—Gordon Allport

- How does this "apostle" contradict himself?
- What are the moral implications of believing anything, except that which is in the Bible?
- Do you believe that a free person should still have some limitations? Explain.
- Do you believe that freedom can be destructive? If so, how?

FAITH CHALLENGE
How Should Christians Respond to the Following Argument?

What makes the Bible so different from any other "holy" book? The Talmud (a holy book of Judaism written by many rabbis) is very similar to the Old Testament—why not obey it just as we do the Bible? Millions of people base their lives on the Book of Mormon. And even the Quran (the holy book of Islam, written by Mohammed) includes many truths from the Bible. It seems that all great religions of the world support the same truths. So why should we follow just what the Bible says and ignore all the other books?

- Do you think it's possible that all truth is God's truth, no matter where it's found? Explain.
- Would it be valuable to study "holy" books from other religions? Why or why not?
- If a Christian friend told you that he or she was going to begin studying the Koran or the Talmud, what would you say to him or her?
- Do you agree or disagree that all great religions support the same truths? Explain.
- Read John 20:30-31 and 2 Peter 2:1-3. How can you tell the difference between a false teaching and a teaching that is from God?
- Read Jeremiah 6:10. How have other religions done what this Scripture reflects? What aspect of Christianity is offensive to them?

How Should Christians Respond to the Following Argument?

The Bible is full of contradictions. In one place it says you can reach heaven only by faith alone; in another, it says you need both faith and good deeds. It has two totally different accounts of creation in the first three chapters of Genesis. And even if those problems can be explained away somehow, there's still the significant problem of the Bible's description of God. In the Old Testament, he's a God of war, who tells his people to slay women and children—even animals. Then in the New Testament, he becomes a God of love and forgiveness. It just doesn't make sense. How can we trust a book like that?

- How would you respond to a friend who held this viewpoint?
- A paradox is a "seeming contradiction." In what ways are these and other "problems" in the Bible paradoxes?
- What would be some possible ways to reconcile these seeming contradictions?
- Read 2 Peter 1:16-21. Would the Holy Spirit intentionally give us contradictory messages? If so, why?
- Did God's character change between the writing of the Old Testament and New Testament? If not, did anything change?

PAIR SHARE

Write the following questions on newsprint or a dry-erase board where everyone can see them. Ask teenagers to form pairs and discuss the questions with their partners.

- How would Christianity be different if we weren't able to trust in the Bible?
- What contribution does the Holy Spirit make in our reading of Scripture?
- Tell your partner about a specific time the Bible really spoke to you personally.

GROUP WORK

Have each person look through the Bible for a prayer that he or she can identify with personally. They can chose prayers for the group or personal prayers. Suggest that they look through the psalms or in the opening verses of Paul's letters. Then have each person read the prayer aloud and briefly explain why it was chosen.

CLOSING

Give each student a copy of the "My Response" handout (p. 80). Encourage youth to write out their prayers in response to God, using the prayer-starter on the handout. Then point out the action plans they can do in response to what they've learned in this lesson.

After time for personal prayer, you may want to finish the lesson with a group prayer.

My Response

Prayer

Dear God: I'm grateful for the miracle of the Bible. Thank you for showing me...

_____

_____

_____

Action Plans

Try these ideas for putting what you've talked about into action.

● To enrich your study of the Bible, select a Scripture to explore in depth, and read it in several versions—The Living Bible, the New American Standard, the King James Version, and the New International Version, for example.

● Design a personal month-long Bible-reading plan. You could arrange it topically, canonically (the order the books appear in the Bible), or chronologically. At the top of a page, write a spiritual objective you hope to accomplish. Then underneath it list how much you intend to read and when. Be realistic. At the end of the month, evaluate whether or not you met your objective and the factors involved. Learn from this initial experience, and use it to help you shape next month's plan.

● Write some of the memory verses in this book and some of your personal favorites on index cards. Carry the cards with you to help you memorize the Scriptures.

● Have people share their favorite Scripture passages and explain why the passages mean so much to them.

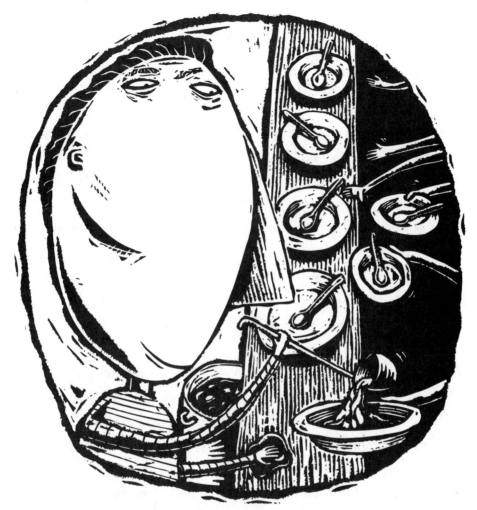

12. How Can I Understand the Bible and Apply It to My Life?

INDIVIDUAL WORK
One Christian Perspective to Think About

I remember the first time the Lord spoke to me powerfully through the Bible. I was on a trip with some Christian friends down by the Texas coast. During the trip one of my friends gave me a card. It was just a note to say how much she enjoyed our friendship. But at the end of the card she wrote a Scripture reference and a note saying that she thought of me whenever she read it. The Scripture was Isaiah 58:14: " 'You will find your joy in the Lord, and I will cause you to ride on the heights of the land and to feast on the inheritance of your father Jacob.' The mouth of the Lord has spoken."

It hit me like a brick between the eyes. The Lord was speaking to me—about my life and my future—personally.

The secret of understanding how to apply the Bible to your life is simply to realize that it isn't just a textbook that teaches you about the nature of life; and it isn't just a book of rules that explains what's right or wrong (even though it does do those things). The Bible is a doorway into a living, real-time relationship with God. God speaks directly to us through the Bible.

So how do we hear him speaking? Before you open the Book, remember that it's OK to be a little selective. Say you open to 1 Chronicles 1:40: "The sons of Shobal: Alvan, Manahath, Ebal, Shepho and Onam. The sons of Zibeon: Aiah and Anah." After reading that verse, it's not impossible, but it might be difficult to walk away thinking, "Wow, God! I never thought of it that way before." Maybe God will speak to you as you randomly open the Bible and start reading, but it never hurts to have a plan of attack.

Is there something you want to know more about? Look it up in a concordance or a topical Bible, and read the corresponding verses. Was last week's sermon good? Make a note of the verses your pastor taught on, and read them again. If you want an even more vigorous plan, buy a daily devotional, and study the recommended Bible readings. If you still don't know where to start, open the Bible to John 1:1, and start reading.

As you read, remember that true understanding of the Bible comes through the Holy Spirit. So ask him to help you understand and apply what you read. It's amazing how the Holy Spirit will bring specific circumstances to mind after you've asked him for some help.

As you continue, spend a little time to reflect on what you've read. When you get to a verse or a passage that's interesting, think about it. Ask God to show you how it applies to your life. When you get to a confusing part, try to make sense of it. If you can't make sense of it, mark it so you can come back to it. Check out what Bible commentaries say about the issue. Ask a friend, a pastor, or a parent what he or she thinks it means. Ask God what it means, and read it again. Ask God to show you how the verse applies to your life.

While reading, you may see that God wants you to take immediate action. For example, if you read, "Honor your father and your mother" (Deuteronomy 5:16); and then realize that you don't honor them, God may be directing you to repent immediately. Sometimes the application of Scripture is a long process. It may take years before you really understand what biblical love really is.

And once you understand the concept, it may take years before you are really able to live it. The important thing is to act on what you do understand while you strive to understand more.

Think about ways you can live out God's Word both immediately and in the future. Ask God to help you to see the world in a different way and to recognize his truth when you run across it. And keep your eyes open. Look for the opportunities God will give you to live out what you read.

God wants to know you. He's provided the Bible as a tool to reach you, to heal you, and to change you. The truth may come in a way that seems almost random. It may also come after long periods (we're talking years) of questions and study. Either way, through the words you will hear God calling. I guarantee it.

My Thoughts, Feelings, and Questions

Write your answers on the back of this paper.
- Read Hebrews 4:12. When have you heard God speak to you very clearly through his Word?
- What areas do you think you should change in your study of the Bible?

Commit It to Memory

"For the word of God is living and active. Sharper than any double-edged sword, it penetrates even to dividing soul and spirit, joints and marrow; it judges the thoughts and attitudes of the heart."—Hebrews 4:12

QUESTIONS TO TALK ABOUT AS A GROUP

When everyone has read the Christian perspective and completed the journaling section, discuss these questions as a group.

- What sources do you depend on to tell you what's true and real about life? Explain.

- What are some obstacles to studying the Bible, either for you or other people?

- If a person has a regular personal Bible reading time, do you think it's still necessary that he or she get input from Christian books and teachers? Why or why not?

- Do you think it's possible to be a dedicated scholar of the Bible and not really know God? Explain.

- Read 2 Timothy 3:14-17. How might this Scripture be applied today?

- In verse 14, the author mentions the importance of Timothy's Christian mentors. What should you look for in a person who teaches the Bible?

SMALL-GROUP WORK

Give each student a copy of the "Faith Challenge" handout (p. 85). Ask youth to form small groups of three to five students. In their groups, have students read the challenging perspectives on the handout and discuss the questions that follow each one.

Jump-Start

If your group discussion needs a jump-start, read the following quotations and discuss the questions as a group.

"Ours would be a better country if people would just obey two of the Ten Commandments. Any two."[1]—Michael Sovern

- Do you agree with this quote? Why or why not?
- Should people pick and chose which parts of the Bible they believe and obey? Explain.
- Do you think it's possible to be a Christian and believe that the Bible, while a very good book, does not have the final authority with regard to moral absolutes? Explain.
- What would you tell a friend who says there are no moral absolutes?

"It is Christ Himself, not the Bible, who is the true word of God. The Bible, read in the right spirit and with the guidance of good teachers, will bring us to Him."[2]—C.S. Lewis

- What do you think Lewis is saying?
- What does Lewis say is the goal of reading the Bible? Do you agree or disagree?
- Do you think that reading any other Christian literature in a similar spirit can also bring us to Christ in the same way the Bible does? Explain.
- What is the "right spirit" in which we should read the Bible?
- What is a "good teacher" to you?

FAITH CHALLENGE
How Should Christians Respond to the Following Argument?

The Bible was written over two thousand years ago. It's a good book, but it simply doesn't apply to life in modern times. The Bible says nothing about most of the issues modern people deal with. How can I take two-thousand-year-old morality and apply it to test-tube babies or homosexual discrimination? It just doesn't make sense to follow the Bible anymore. It was OK once upon a time, but it's irrelevant today.

● Do you agree or disagree with this perspective? Explain.

● What topics or issues do you face today that you think the Bible doesn't address?

● Does the Bible intend to address every single aspect of human existence? Explain.

● Read Matthew 24:35 and Romans 15:4. What would you say to a friend who believes the Bible is outdated and irrelevant?

● How can we know what God thinks about a certain issue if it's not explicitly addressed in the Bible?

How Should Christians Respond to the Following Argument?

Truth is relative. It depends on the situation you face and your own heart. The Bible contains a lot of good advice, but you have to filter it through your own experiences to determine what you should keep and what you should throw away. For example, a lot of the people who wrote the Bible had cultural hang-ups that I don't believe in. They also wrote that God is love, but then claimed that he punishes "sinners" by sending them to hell.

Well, I believe God is love; but my definition of love is bigger than theirs. God's love is so big that he would never send anyone to hell. So the Bible has some great truths in it, but you can't blindly accept everything you read as "God's Word." Some of it is, and some of it isn't.

● How do you think people who hold this viewpoint decide what's wrong and what's right?

● Take this viewpoint to its logical conclusion. What would a purely relativistic society look like?

● Read Deuteronomy 4:2. Why would God command this?

PAIR SHARE

Write the following questions on newsprint or a dry-erase board where everyone can see them. Ask teenagers to form pairs and discuss the questions with their partners.

● What current issues are you facing that you need the Bible to guide you in?

● What are some of the "mental blocks," or obstacles, you have when it comes to personal Bible study?

● Tell your partner about the disciplines, techniques, and tools for Bible study you've used in the past that have helped you connect with God. Encourage each other to try new disciplines that can enrich your time with God in his Word.

GROUP WORK

Ask the person on your right about a specific Scripture or concept in the Bible that he or she would like to apply. Then pray aloud for that person, asking God to show him or her how to apply that biblical concept.

CLOSING

Give each student a copy of the "My Response" handout (p. 87). Encourage youth to write out their prayers in response to God, using the prayer-starter on the handout. Then point out the action plans they can do in response to what they've learned in this lesson.

After time for personal prayer, you may want to finish the lesson with a group prayer.

MY RESPONSE
Prayer

Dear God: Thank you for the written history of redemption and grace that we have in the Bible. Help me to...

_____

_____

_____

ACTION PLANS

Try these ideas for putting what you've talked about into action.

● If you're having a difficult time understanding a passage of Scripture, borrow a Bible commentary or dictionary from your church library or your pastor. Some Bibles are even published with supplemental study aides that can greatly enhance your personal study. They can be bought at your local Christian bookstore.

● If you're "stuck in a rut" during your Bible-reading time, try something you haven't done before. For instance, read a Christian biography or novel, use a new devotional book, read stories from the Old Testament, or do a character study.

● God speaks through his Word, but he also speaks through the events in your life. Before reading the Bible, ask God to help you see the connection between real life and his will for you as revealed in Scripture.

● Have everyone read the same Scripture passage (such as Psalm 1) and then silently think about how they might apply it to their lives individually. After a few minutes, have people share their insights with the rest of the group. Encourage everyone to be very specific. They might even share a story about a situation in the past when they could have applied (or actually did apply) the Scripture.

"SER COMO EL PERICO, QUE DICE LO QUE SABE, PERO NO SABE LO QUE DICE."

"To be like the parakeet, that says what he knows but doesn't know what he says."[3]

—Spanish Proverb

13. How Can I Hear God Communicate to Me?

INDIVIDUAL WORK
One Christian Perspective to Think About

Almost three years ago, I faced a huge decision. We lived in Michigan and had a nice home we had built for ourselves out in the country. My kids had a horse, two dogs, two cats, a rabbit, and a guinea pig. My older son was in high school, and we were settling into the community. Then I was offered a job in Colorado. Although the news was exciting, I didn't know if I was prepared to leave my job and our new home and move my family 1,200 miles away. I really wasn't sure what God was telling me to do.

When I have a big decision to make, I find myself seeking communication from God much more desperately than at any other time. That's not to say that such a pattern is appropriate, but I'd guess it's pretty common. When we feel like we really need a word from God before we proceed with some course of action, how do we get it? Why doesn't God just drop us a note and let us know precisely what we should do?

I don't have perfect answers to those questions, but here are a few of the principles I've found to be important in hearing God communicate to me.

God communicates through the Bible. The pages of Scripture contain the basis of God's communication with humans. There we find hundreds of principles that can help us live wise, faithful, loving lives here on earth. And we find the words and teachings that can lead us to eternal life. But we won't find God saying in Scripture, "You should quit your job in Michigan and move to Colorado." So how do we really get communication from the Bible on specific topics the Bible doesn't address?

The principle of familiarity comes into play here. In case you haven't heard of the principle of familiarity, it says, "The more familiar you are with someone, the more likely you are to figure out what that person would say about a particular issue." So to apply that principle, the better we know God, the more likely we'll be able to figure out what he wants to say to us. And the way to get to know God better is to spend time studying his message to us—the Bible.

Another way God communicates to us through the Bible is with the help of the Holy Spirit. Jesus said that he would give us the Holy Spirit to teach us and help us remember his teachings (see John 14:26). As we're seeking to hear from God, the Holy Spirit may guide us to just the right passage— just what God wants us to hear from him. For example, a pastor at church may give you a message on loving others just when you're having a hard time caring about a troubled kid at school. Or when you're struggling with something, the Holy Spirit can bring to your mind a passage of Scripture you've studied or memorized in the past—a perfect message for the situation you're facing.

Sometimes a message may come from God in the form of a "gentle whisper" (1 Kings 19:12). It may be just a thought occurring in your head. However, we must be careful not to place too much confidence in such a voice, because it's really hard to tell whether it's coming from God, our own minds, or from a wrong outside influence.

God has communicated with us through Jesus. In the first chapter of the Gospel of John, we learn that Jesus is the word of God with skin. Jesus lived God's message to us while he was on earth. As we read about Jesus' life and teachings, and develop our relationship with God through him, we understand more of what God might want to say to us. We'll also learn more about how he wants us to live.

God communicates with us through his faithful followers. One reason God created the church is so Christians would have other people to go to for encouragement, sharing, and counsel. This method of hearing from God is trickier than the first two. Christians we know well and respect for their closeness to God can often give us advice that God would want us to hear. And if two or more such faithful followers give us similar advice, it's a pretty good bet that God's message is coming through. However, two Christians we admire and trust may give us differing advice. At such times we may need to seek out more counsel and be careful to listen for what we think God might be telling us—not just for what we'd like to hear.

God can communicate with us through circumstances. This method is probably the least reliable, but one that we can throw into the mix. When we're seeking to hear from God, sometimes things happening around us can be his message to us. For example, if you think God wants you to become a doctor, but seventeen medical schools have turned you down, God may be telling you to think again. However, we need to be careful not to let only circumstances guide us. God's communication through the Bible, the Holy Spirit, and other Christians is much more trustworthy.

God has given us the ability to think and reason. He wants us to use that ability to understand what communication we receive is really from him. If I felt that God told me that he wants me to jump in front of oncoming traffic in order to show him my great faith, it would probably be a good idea to take a minute to think and reason before I act. I should think about how such a decision would bring glory to God. I should think about whether such a decision lines up with other biblical principles such as God's command not to test him. I should think of the consequences of my actions for myself and for others. Of course, there are times when we must act against our reason by taking steps of faith. But acting in faith is quite different than acting foolishly.

My Thoughts, Feelings, and Questions

Write your answers on the back of this paper.
- What's confusing to you about the way God communicates to us?
- Read Isaiah 30:21. What do you think God's voice sounds like?

Commit It to Memory

"Whether you turn to the right or to the left, your ears will hear a voice behind you saying, 'This is the way; walk in it.'"—Isaiah 30:21

QUESTIONS TO TALK ABOUT AS A GROUP

When everyone has read the Christian perspective and completed the journaling section, discuss these questions as a group.

● Have you ever been desperate for God to speak to you? Describe a time when you felt that way.

● Has God ever spoken to you? If so, when? If so, how?

● How does God communicate to us?

● How can we know the difference between God telling us something and our own desires?

● Read 1 Kings 19:11-13. What does this passage suggest about the way God communicates with people?

● If your best friend said that God told him or her to quit school and become a foreign missionary, what counsel would you give?

SMALL-GROUP WORK

Give each student a copy of the "Faith Challenge" handout (p. 92). Ask youth to form small groups of three to five students. In their groups, have students read the challenging perspectives on the handout and discuss the questions that follow each one.

Jump-Start

If your group discussion needs a jump-start, read the following quotations and discuss the questions as a group.

"If God has spoken, why is the universe not convinced?"[1]—Percy Bysshe Shelley

● What is Shelley saying?
● Do you think God has spoken to the universe? Explain.
● Why do you think people want so desperately to hear from God?

"In the past God spoke to our forefathers through the prophets at many times and in various ways, but in these last days he has spoken to us by his Son."—Hebrews 1:1-2a

● What methods does God use to speak to us today?
● How has God spoken to us by his Son?
● Why doesn't everyone listen to what God has said?

FAITH CHALLENGE
How Should Christians Respond to the Following Argument?

God communicates to us through angels or spirit guides. People can become channels through which angels or other spirits speak to deliver messages from God or the spirit world. We can contact angels, know them by name, and develop relationships with them; thus gaining an inside track for special spiritual advice and wisdom that no one else has.

● Have you ever heard someone describe an experience like this? What would you say if a friend told you about a similar experience?

● What do you think is attractive about this belief?

● Does God communicate to us through angels?

● Read Colossians 2:18-19 and 2 Corinthians 11:13-15. What do you think these verses say about angelic encounters?

● How can we tell whether supernatural experiences are from God?

How Should Christians Respond to the Following Argument?

No one can know God or even know if there is a God. If there is a God, he has given no evidence of his existence and no direct revelation. God may or may not exist, but there is no possibility of communication with a being that is unknowable, even if he does exist. If God exists, what prevents him from making his "revelations" simple and clear by speaking in an audible voice? And why would a God who created everyone only speak to a select few? God doesn't tell humans what to do. Humans use God as an excuse to tell others what to do.

● How would you respond to this argument?

● Read Isaiah 40:6-31. What does this Scripture say about God's communication with people?

● How does human understanding limit our ability to comprehend God?

● Why doesn't God make it clear that he exists by yelling it out to the universe or by showing himself to us?

PAIR SHARE

Write the following questions on newsprint or a dry-erase board where everyone can see them. Ask teenagers to form pairs and discuss the questions with their partners.

- When it comes to hearing God's voice, how much responsibility do you think lies with you? with God?
- Tell your partner about an area of your life where you need God's direction. Help each other think of ways you can find God's direction and make the right decision.

GROUP WORK

Pray aloud for the person on your right, asking God to help that person find God's direction in his or her life.

CLOSING

Give each student a copy of the "My Response" handout (p. 94). Encourage youth to write out their prayers in response to God, using the prayer-starter on the handout. Then point out the action plans they can do in response to what they've learned in this lesson.

After time for personal prayer, you may want to finish the lesson with a group prayer.

My Response
Prayer

Dear God: Help me to hear your voice. Give me your direction in…

_____

_____

_____

Action Plans

Try these ideas for putting what you've talked about into action.

● Spend five minutes just listening to God.

● When you face a decision, a challenge, or a concern, try going to all the sources listed in "One Christian Perspective to Think About" to find God's direction.

● Make a list of all the ways you have seen God communicate to you. Be on the lookout for God's direction and his voice during the week. Be prepared to share your experiences at the next meeting.

● Seek counsel from someone else in the group to help you find God's direction. Be sure to check the Bible to make sure what he or she says is true.

**"God has revealed many truths which He has not explained. We will just have to be content to let Him know some things we do not and take Him at His word."[2]
—B.A. Copass**

Endnotes

Introduction

1. *The Treasury of Religious & Spiritual Quotations: Words to Live By* (Pleasantville, NY: The Reader's Digest Association, Inc., 1994), ed. Rebecca Davison and Susan Mesner, 177.

Lesson 1

1. Max Anders, *God: Knowing Our Creator* (Nashville: Thomas Nelson, Inc., 1995), 6.
2. *The International Thesaurus of Quotations* (New York: Thomas Y. Crowell Company, Inc., 1970), comp. Rhoda Thomas Tripp, 249.
3. *The Encyclopedia of Religious Quotations* (Westwood, NJ: Fleming H. Revell Company, 1965), ed. Frank S. Mead, 168.
4. Antony Fernando with Leonard Swidler, *Buddhism Made Plain: An Introduction for Christians and Jews* (Maryknoll, New York: Orbis Books, 1985), 104-106.

Lesson 2

1. Michael D. Warden, "Creation and Evolution," *Why Creation Matters,* Core Belief Bible Study Series (Loveland, CO: Group Publishing, Inc., 1997), 23.
2. *The Treasury of Religious & Spiritual Quotations* (Pleasantville, NY: The Reader's Digest Association, Inc., 1994), ed. Rebecca Davison and Susan Mesner, 113.
3. Ibid., 115.
4. Michael D. Warden, "Creation and Evolution," *Why Creation Matters*, Core Belief Bible Study Series (Loveland, CO: Group Publishing, Inc., 1997), 22.

Lesson 3

1. Stephen Parolini, "Buddha and Mohammed—Why Not?" *Why Jesus Christ Matters*, Core Belief Bible Study Series (Loveland, CO: Group Publishing, Inc., 1995), 32.
2. Douglas Groothuis, *Confronting the New Age* (Downers Grove, IL: Intervarsity Press, 1988), 118-125.
3. Walter Martin, *The Kingdom of the Cults* (Minneapolis: Bethany House Publishers, 1985), 378.
4. *The Encyclopedia of Religious Quotations,* 49.
5. Douglas Groothuis, *Revealing the New Age Jesus* (Downers Grove, IL: Intervarsity Press, 1990), 15-19.
6. Ron Rhodes, *The Culting of America* (Eugene, OR: Harvest House Publishers, 1994), 74.

Lesson 4

1. *The Treasury of Religious & Spiritual Quotations*, 118.

Lesson 5

1. *The Treasury of Religious & Spiritual Quotations*, 505.
2. Malise Ruthven, *Islam in the World* (New York and Oxford: Oxford University Press, 1984), 82-85.
3. John Bartlett, *Bartlett's Familiar Quotations* (New York: Little, Brown & Company, 1992), 124.10.

Lesson 6

1. *The Quest Study Bible,* New International Version (Grand Rapids, MI: The Zondervan Corporation, 1994), 1350.
2. *Bartlett's Familiar Quotations,* 100.11.
3. George A. Mather and Larry A. Nichols, *Dictionary of Cults, Sects, Religions and the Occult* (Grand Rapids, MI: Zondervan Publishing House, 1993), 120.
4. *Bartlett's Familiar Quotations,* 212.13.
5. Ibid., 299.4.
6. Ibid., 420.13.

Lesson 7

1. *Truths That Transform* (Old Tappan, NJ: Fleming H. Revell Company, 1974), 122.
2. *12,000 Religious Quotations* (Grand Rapids, MI: Baker Book House), ed. Frank S. Mead, 224.

Lesson 8

1. *Bartlett's Familiar Quotations,* 495.1.
2. Colin Chapman, *The Case for Christianity* (Grand Rapids, MI: William B. Eerdman's Publishing Co., 1981), 60.
3. Polly Young-Eisendrath, *The Gifts of Suffering* (Reading, MA: Addison-Wesley Publishing Company, Inc.), 13.
4. Ibid., 12-14.
5. *The Treasury of Religions & Spiritual Quotations,* 540.

Lesson 9

1. Billy Graham, *The Holy Spirit: Activating God's Power in Your Life* (Waco, TX: Word Books, 1978), 16-21, 37-38.
2. *Rise & Shine* (Portland, OR: Multnomah Press, 1989), 81.

Lesson 10

1. Terry Law, *The Truth About Angels* (Orlando, FL: Creation House, 1994), 135.
2. *12,000 Religious Quotations*, 109.
3. Duane A. Garrett, *Angels and the New Spirituality* (Nashville: Broadman & Holman Publishers, 1995), 133.

Lesson 11

1. Lisa Baba Lauffer, "The Making of the Bible," *The Truth About the Bible,* Core Belief Bible Study Series (Loveland, CO: Group Publishing, Inc., 1997), 23.
2. *The Expositor's Bible Commentary, Volume 1* (Grand Rapids, MI: Zondervan Publishing House, 1979), ed. Frank E. Gaebelein, 421.
3. Group Magazine (July/August 1996), 17.
4. *Quotations of Wit & Wisdom,* ed. John W. Gardner and Francesca Gardner Reese, 102.

Lesson 12

1. Roy L. Stewart, *Quotations With an Attitude* (New York: Sterling Publishing Company, Inc., 1995), 108.
2. Wayne Martindale and Jerry Root, *The Quotable Lewis* (Wheaton, IL: Tyndale House Publishers, Inc., 1989), 72.
3. *Quotations of Wit & Wisdom*, 231.

Lesson 13

1. *12,000 Religious Quotations*, 381.
2. Ibid., 451.